Before the

Revolution

St. Petersburg in Photographs: 1890-1914

MIKHAIL P. IROSHNIKOV,
YURY B. SHELAYEV, LIUDMILA A. PROTSAI

FOREWORD BY JAMES H. BILLINGTON
Librarian of Congress

INTRODUCTION BY DMITRY S. LIKHACHOV
Member of the Academy of Sciences of the U.S.S.R.

HARRY N. ABRAMS, INC., PUBLISHERS, NEW YORK
NAUKA PUBLISHERS, LENINGRAD
JV SMART, LENINGRAD

Translated from the Russian by Evgueni Filippov

Editors: Mark D. Markin, Alexander S. Turundayevsky,
Mark D. Greenberg
Designer: Alexander V. Lobanov

Photographs from the original negatives have been provided by the Leningrad Central State Archive of Cinema
and Photo Documents

Library of Congress Cataloging-in-Publication Data

Iroshnikov, Mikhail Pavlovich.
  Before the revolution: St. Petersburg in photographs, 1890—1914/
Mikhail P. Iroshnikov, Yury B. Shelayev, Liudmila A. Protsai;
Foreword by James H. Billington; introduction by Dmitry S. Likhachov
      p.   cm.
ISBN 0-8109-3813-8
  1. Leningrad (R.S.F.S.R.) — History — To 1917 — Pictorial works.
2. Leningrad (R.S.F.S.R.) — Description — Views. 3. Leningrad
(R.S.F.S.R.) — Social life and customs — Pictorial works.
I. Shelayev, Yury B.   II. Protsai, Liudmila A.   III. Billington, James H.
IV. Title.
DK568.I76 1991
947'.47083—dc20   90-23438
                                                CIP

Published in the United States by Harry N. Abrams,
Incorporated, New York
A Times Mirror Company

Printed and bound in Finland

Contents

ST. PETERSBURG AS SEEN
BY THE CAMERA'S LENS
by James H. Billington

This is a remarkable, in many ways unique, pictorial record of one of the world's great cities — one that both attracts and eludes description.

The city is not even sure of its name. The informative text, written in the Soviet Union, provided for these pictures calls it Petersburg, thereby making it clear that we are not being given just another historically distorted retrospective look at early Leningrad — as if the city's identity were defined by the leader of the Revolution that followed the period depicted here. But its formal name was St. Petersburg (changed to the more Slavic Petrograd in 1914; which continued throughout Lenin's lifetime); and its popular designation was Peter.

Peter the Great, who founded the city in 1703, made it the capital of Imperial Russia in 1712 and saw in it not just a window to the West but a rival to Rome and even a new Jerusalem. On the other hand, the members of the great literary culture who blossomed in and wrote about the city saw it as the new Babylon. It was a place of vast public spaces built for parades more than for people. The pedestrian little people of Russian literature were intimidated by larger-than-life statues of emperors on horseback. Periodic floods pouring from the northern wastes into the Gulf of Finland were invariably seen as biblical judgments by Russian traditionalists. Solzhenitsyn has called the city either Nevagrad, or "swamp city," which is close to the earliest names given to the site by Finnish fishermen, who had previously camped there even as they scorned it as unfit for permanent habitation.

The city depicted here is not, however, simply a composite of the two familiar images that history has left us. It is not just the imperial center of great Baroque and Neoclassical architectural ensembles spiced with hints of the haunted, inhuman city of the literary imagination. Both of these images frequently intrude into this photographic record of the city at the turn of this century. But the dominant image that such an encyclopedic record of black-and-white photography gives us is one of human vitality and a certain sense of hopefulness amidst social change and dramatic incongruities.

In these pictures, we see the mythological lions and eagles, classical gods, and tsarist statues that adorned the roofs, triumphal arches, and granite columns of the capital of the world's largest empire. But beneath them, at ground level, we also see bustling and diverse ordinary people going about a variety of practical tasks in a period of rising living standards and social expectations. One also sees and almost feels the surrounding cold (in a location parallel to the northernmost tip of Labrador) and the all-permeating dampness.

Photography can be the realistic medium par excellence. So it is perhaps appropriate that this photographic record of an emerging, bourgeois Petersburg seems to illustrate an identity described by the founder of Russian realistic criticism, Vissarion Belinsky. Writing more than a half century before these pictures were taken, Belinsky saw in Petersburg something more than the official city built largely by the Empresses Elizabeth and Catherine II in the past century, and more than the emerging home of the unofficial intelligentsia Belinsky was helping to establish. To Belinsky, Petersburg was "a new city in an old country" that had become "a mighty oak, which concentrates in itself all the living juices of Russia." It was a city that "does not believe in words, it requires activity."

These pictures record the vitality and variety of that activity in the last days of Petersburg. They record *la vie quotidienne* of the city at a time of rapid economic growth, rising reformist agitation, and extraordinary cultural experimentation. Moscow was just passing Petersburg as the largest city of the realm — and would replace it as the capital after World War I led to revolution and civil war. Under its new name of Leningrad, the city suffered unmercifully at the hands first of Stalin in the purges, then of Hitler in the blockade of World War II. If most of the inner city was saved and some of its spectacular surrounding buildings restored, the city we see today is not the dynamic place of rapid change and multiple possibilities that existed in the late imperial period and that is faithfully depicted in these photographs.

We see here the documented urban history of new technologies used in bridges, Art Nouveau introduced in commercial buildings, the growth of a more open economy. We see people exuberantly crossing the bridges, buildings seeking to assert individuality on Nevsky Prospekt, and the teeming variety of both the people and the languages and typography of commercial signs in Gostiny Dvor.

It is both the world of old family photographs that we recognize, and another world, which we can never understand. There was, even in cosmopolitan Petersburg, far greater ethnic uniformity than in any great American city. Fully 85 percent of the population was Great Russian and 75 percent of it was male. As the mecca of military and civil officials became a manufacturing and commercial city, it depended on seasonal workers who often left their families behind in the countryside. Hence, the predominance of men in the pictorial record.

There is more than a little indication here of the genuine affection with which the tsarist tradition and the Orthodox Church were regarded even in this most Westernized and secularized corner of the Russian Empire. We see, along with worldly concerns, repeated pictures of ordinary people enjoying often in informal ways the processions of the Church and the celebrations in 1913 of the three-hundredth anniversary of the establishment of the Romanov dynasty. At the same time, we see the barrack-like housing of the male work force and the sweatshops where women were beginning to enter the work force. Finally, there is the emerging world in between: an amorphous middle layer in which a declining nobility and a rising bourgeoisie were trying to reform the old autocracy. We see pictures of the closest approximations to a real parliament that were also produced in the Petersburg of this era.

These pictures give a particularly vivid sense of the way in which old and new technologies were competing in a time of change. We see the variety of styles in popular sleighs and aristocratic carriages that were competing for the transportation business at the very time that automobiles and trolley cars were also coming onto the scene. And we see sailboats, barges, steamboats, and warships, clogging the waterways around this Baltic seaport and naval base. The central point in the city, which Dostoyevsky called "the most abstract and intentional" of all urban complexes, was the Admiralty, and its symbol (like that of the famed Cathedral of Saints Peter and Paul) was not a dome over land, but a spire by the water.

Amidst all the specificity of a time and place, great photography occasionally captures archetypes as well — as in the picture of a lone boy in the snow with his hat askew or of the ruler alone and somehow very small on a balcony when seen from afar.

So this book is not just decoration for a coffee table, but a record to be studied and savored on many levels. It is for black-and-white photography a record of the capital that is almost as remarkable as the contemporaneous record of the empire as a whole that was taken in color photography by order of the tsar, now in the Library of Congress's Prokhudin-Gorsky collection. The record is so lifelike that one longs for the accompanying sounds (the mixture of bands and bells with industrial construction, of wind in open spaces and the crunch of leaves in parks) and even the smells — of sea air mixed with the aroma of horse manure from the old days and of gasoline fumes from the new.

This record includes some examples of buildings subsequently destroyed by mindless Soviet planners, but the extent of such needless destruction is not adequately conveyed since the focus in this collection is on the more familiar buildings that have survived. It is a tribute to old Petersburg that one of its last survivors, the octogenarian scholar of Old Russia, Dmitry Likhachov of Leningrad, has become the leader of the resurgent movement for the fuller restoration of historic buildings in the USSR today.

No record in any medium can bring back the past in all its fullness. And no one can say what was the true identity — or even the most appropriate name — for this unique city during this Indian summer of its imperial past. But all will be grateful for this rich record of what it was and what its people were doing in the period of ferment and change at the beginning of this century before they were swept into the grim new world of total war and totalitarian peace.

THE PETERSBURG OF MY CHILDHOOD
by Dmitry S. Likhachov

Petersburg and Leningrad are different cities. Not in everything, of course. Some similarities remain, but they only underline the differences.

My early childhood impressions are of barges, barges, barges. They were all over the Neva River, and its branches and canals. Laden with firewood and bricks, were unloaded by laborers the barges onto wheelbarrows, which they rolled along strips of iron onto the bank. The grating that borders the embankment was open in many places and in some places had been removed altogether. The bricks were taken away at once, while firewood was put in stacks on the embankment and then loaded onto carts for delivery to the firewood markets that were situated all over the city, on the canals and on the two Nevka rivers. Although you could buy it in any season, it was autumn when everyone really stocked up on firewood. Long poles were used to propel the barges along the canals. It was fascinating to watch two husky lads in bast shoes (they were less prone to slip and were much cheaper than boots) walking along the sides of the barge from bow to stern, resting their shoulders on the pole, and pushing the barges. Their job complete, they returned from the stern to the bow, one end of the pole dragging across the water.

On the Lebiazhya Kanavka (Swan Ditch) near the Summer Garden huge boats unloaded pottery — pots, plates, mugs, sometimes toys, the most popular being clay whistles. Occasionally wooden spoons were sold. All these wares were brought from Lake Onega.

Boats and barges rocked gently. The Neva flowed by, swaying the masts of schooners, the barges, the rowboats that took you across the Neva for a kopeck, and the tugs that tilted their funnels as they passed under the bridges. There was a whole forest of swaying masts at the Krestovsky Bridge on the Bolshaya Nevka and near the Tuchkov Bridge on the Malaya Nevka.

Everything in the city seemed to sway and roll. A ride in a horse cab or in a sled was shaky. Crossing the Neva in a rowboat was shaky. Riding over the cobblestones shook you to pieces. But once you reached the flagstone pavement — along the "royal route" from the Winter Palace to the Tsarskoye Selo Station, on Nevsky Prospekt, on Bolshaya Morskaya and Malaya Morskaya streets, or in front of the stately homes — the riding was smooth and noiseless.

Most of the public buildings were dark red. The glass windows shone against the red walls. The windows were well washed, and there were many mirror-like shop windows, which cracked during the siege of Leningrad. The Winter Palace, the General Staff, and the Headquarters of the Guards were all dark red. The Senate and the Synod were red. Hundreds of other buildings — barracks, warehouses, government offices — were also red. The walls of the Lithuanian Castle were red. This hideous transit prison was the same color as the palace. Only the Admiralty defied the rule by being yellow and white. The other buildings were also well painted in dark colors. But you could not really see the buildings. You could not see the river or the canals. You could not see the façades behind the notices and ads. The tram wires were carefully placed in order not to "intrude on property": they were not attached to walls but were supported by poles that took up a lot of street space, and not just the ordinary streets, but even Nevsky Prospekt itself was hidden by the tram poles, ads, and notices. They climbed as high as the third floor. They swamped Liteiny and Vladimirsky Prospekts, the center of the city. Some of the ads were attractive. Only the squares were bereft of ads, which made them look even larger and more deserted. Above the pavement in the small streets were pretzels, golden cow heads, gigantic pince-nez, jumbo-sized boots or scissors, all advertising various emporia. Awnings with metal supports spanned the sidewalks. There were rows of posts along the pavement. In front of many old buildings there were, instead of posts, barrels of ancient guns placed upright in the ground. The posts and the guns protected pedestrians from being run over by horse-drawn carts and cabs. But all this obscured the view of the street, as did the kerosene-lamp posts. The lampmen climbed ladders to light, put out, fill, and clean the lamps.

On numerous church and tsarist holidays tricolor flags were put up. In Bolshaya Morskaya and Malaya Morskaya streets the flags hung from ropes strung across the street.

The ground floors on the main streets were a feast for the eye. The main doors were spick-and-span. They had shining copper handles (which were removed in the 1920s to provide copper for the Volkhov Power Dam). The pavements were well swept. There were green kegs or buckets under the drainpipes to keep rainwater from spilling out onto the pavements. The janitors in white aprons emptied the kegs and buckets. Every once in a while a doorman in gold-embroidered navy blue livery emerged for a breath of fresh air — there were doormen not only in palaces, but in the entrances of many apartment houses.

The gleaming shop windows were particularly exciting, especially for children, who tugged at their mothers' sleeves, pulling them toward the windows of toy shops, which displayed tin soldiers and steam engines with carriages on rails. One of the most interesting shops was Doinikov's in the Gostiny Dvor shopping arcade on Nevsky Prospekt, famous for its wide choice of tin soldiers. Standing in the window of pharmacies were large vases with colored liquids: green, blue, yellow, and red. In the evening lamps were lit behind these vases, and the pharmacies could be seen from far away.

Some of the most expensive shops were on the "sunny side" of Nevsky Prospekt ("the sunny side" was almost an official way of referring to the even-numbered houses on that avenue). I remember the windows of the cultured-diamond shop called Teta. In the middle of the window was a contraption with rotating lamps: the diamonds glittered and shimmered in their light.

Where there are now asphalt sidewalks, there were once sidewalks of limestone, while the pavement was made from cobblestones. Limestone slabs were hard to make and costly but they looked beautiful, not as beautiful, though, as the huge granite slabs on Nevsky Prospekt, which can still be seen on the Anichkov Bridge. Many of them have been moved to St. Isaac's Cathedral. In the outskirts, the pavement was sometimes made from wooden boards. They have been described by many writers. They were beautiful and convenient, but during the flood of 1924, being wooden, they floated and caused many casualties by knocking people off their feet and dragging them along with the current. Outside Petersburg, in the provinces, there were often gutters under the wooden pavement, and when the boards became worn, one could fall into the gutter. But not in Petersburg, where there were never gutters under the boards. The cobblestones had to be kept clean and repaired. During the

summer workers came to mend the cobblestones and lay new ones. They prepared the sand grounding, packing it by hand, and then drove in each cobblestone with heavy hammers. They sat while they worked. They had their feet and left hand swathed in cloth to protect them from accidental hammer blows. One could not look at these workers without pity. And yet they did a thorough job, adjusting stone to stone, flat side up — they were real craftsmen. The cobblestone pavements in St. Petersburg were particularly beautiful because they were made from polished granite stones; I liked them especially when they were wet after rain or after being washed.

The sounds of Petersburg! One remembers first of all the clatter of hoofs on the cobblestones. Even Pushkin wrote about the "Bronze Horseman" thundering along the pavement.

The hoofs of the cab horses made a tender sound. Boys could skillfully imitate the sound by clicking their tongues when they played at horses — the favorite pastime of our childhood. The makers of films with period settings try to reproduce the sound of hoofs, but I'm not sure that they know that this sound was different in rainy and dry weather. I remember that each autumn, when we arrived from our dacha at Kuokkala and came out of the Finland Station onto the adjoining square, the place reverberated with the "wet clatter" of hoofs. Then there was the soft rustling sound of wheels rolling over wood blocks and the clatter of hoofs on the same blocks once you crossed the Liteiny Bridge. The cabbies shouted warnings to jaywalkers. The carters goaded their horses on by swinging the end of the reins with a sucking sound. The newspaper vendors called out the names of newspapers, and during World War I they shouted out the news headlines.

Steamers hooted on the Neva, but there was no shouting through the mouthpieces so characteristic of the Volga — apparently it was banned in Petersburg. Little Finnish Shipping Line steamers with open engines chugged along the Fontanka. One could see the stokers and hear the hissing and swishing sound of steam and the captains' commands.

One of the most common sounds in Petersburg's streets before World War I was the jingling of tram bells. I could distinguish four kinds of bell. The first was rung before the tram started. The conductor — before the war invariably a uniformed man — came out from the rear platform at every stop, let all the passengers embark, then stepped on the platform and pulled on a rope connected to a bell in the driver's cab. After getting this signal, the driver started the tram. The rope ran the whole length of the carriage and was attached to a metal bar from which hung leather loops for passengers to hold. The conductor could ring the bell from any place in the tram. This was the second type of bell. The driver had another bell operated by a pedal, which he used to warn passersby. That insistent bell was heard constantly in the streets where trams ran. Later, electric bells came into being. For a long time there were both pedal- and hand-operated electric bells. The conductor's chest was festooned with rolls of paper tickets of different colors. There were tickets that gave you a ride for sections of the route, and there were white transfer tickets for travel on other routes. All these routes could be found in the old guide to Petersburg. When a section of the route ended, and new tickets had to be bought, the conductor would yell: "Yellow tickets stop!" or "Green tickets stop!" or "Red tickets stop!" I will remember the inflection of his voice to the end of my days: I took the tram to go to school every day.

Another frequently heard sound was that of military bands: a regiment marching to church on a Sunday or holiday, a general's funeral, the daily changing of the guard at the Winter Palace by the Preobrazhensky and Semionovsky regiments. Boys flocked to the sounds of the band. It was particular fun when troops returned from the cemetery after a funeral: on such occasions the bands played merry music. Brisk marches were played when the troops went to church, though not, of course, during Lent. Softer sounds came from the spurs on the servicemen's boots. Officers were very particular about the kind of sound their spurs made. The spurs were often silver.

Along and just off Nevsky Prospekt, especially at Gostiny Dvor at the corner of Nevsky Prospekt and Sadovaya (Garden) Street, children could buy balloons: red, green, blue, yellow. The biggest balloons were white, and they had roosters painted on them. The vendors were always surrounded by crowds. You could see them from afar because of the clusters of colored balloons over their heads.

In my time *sbiten* was no longer sold, but my father remembered it and liked to tell me about it. Very bracing, especially in frosty weather, *sbiten* was a mixture of hot water with honey and spices, most often cinnamon. The *sbiten* vendor wrapped his samovar in padded cloth and carried it on his back so that the tap was under his left elbow.

Since not everyone had a clock or a watch, the wail of factory sirens calling people to work wafted from the outskirts in the morning, especially from the Vyborg Side of town. Every factory had a different siren. The sound was alarming and somehow disturbing.

As a child, I had an itch to look inside the houses, but I usually had to content myself with the stories of grown-ups. The shops, of course, I remember. My mother took me to the Colonial Goods store (coffee, tea, cinnamon, and the like), the grocer's, the Surov Shop for cloth and thread, the baker's, the confectionery, and the stationery shops. The salesmen were called *prikazchiki*, or shop assistants. I remember the well-trained shop assistants in the butter shops. They stood a few inches away from the counter with their hands behind their backs. When the customer entered, the shop assistant took one step toward him and let his hands drop. In spite of himself, the customer just had to approach him. You were allowed to taste butter and cheese from the tip of a long knife.

The early cinemas: few people remember the Mirage Cinema on narrow Ofitserskaya (Officers') Street opposite our house; it was constructed from several shops joined together. On Saturdays the whole family went to the Soleil Cinema on Nevsky Prospekt. It was in the same building as the Passage, just off Sadovaya Street. That cinema had been converted from several separate apartments. In addition to the main attraction (I remember *Napoleon's One Hundred Days* and *The Sinking of the Titanic*, a documentary that the cameraman had filmed on the ship; he continued to film the shipwreck until the lights went out, and he went on to shoot in the lifeboat) there were comedies (starring Max Linder, Maciste, and others) and "landscape" films, in which the frames were often hand-painted in bright colors: red, green (for plants), blue (for the sky).

Once we went to a cinema in Nevsky Prospekt; it was

called Parisian or Piccadilly, I think. I was struck by the ushers who wore livery and perhaps even wigs. My parents often took me to the Mariinsky Theatre where they had two seats permanently reserved in a dress-circle box. These shows were — and were meant to be — great occasions. The ladies displayed their jewelry. They sat in the front rows in the boxes and fanned themselves, not because it was hot, but to show off their diamonds. During the ballets the lights were only half-dimmed. Kshesinskaya burst onto the stage all glittering with diamonds. Swaggering officers usually came for the second act. During the intermissions they tried to get everybody to look at them by standing near the orchestra pit, and after the performance they stood ogling the ladies at the entrance. The first ballet I ever saw was *The Nutcracker*. My strongest impression was of falling snow — in a warm hall!

On Good Friday and for Easter matins we went to Pochtamtskaya Street, to the church of the Postal and Telegraph Authority where my father was the head of a "desk," or department. We left our coats in the cloakroom and ascended to the second floor. The parquet floors in the church were well polished. Electric lamps were hidden behind the cornice. The icon lamps were also electric, a fact frowned upon by some parishioners. My father, however, was proud of the novelty — it was his idea. When a family entered, an attendant promptly brought chairs so that they could rest whenever the liturgy permitted. Later I learned that the Nabokov family went to the same church, so I must have met Vladimir Nabokov. He was older than I.

Social inequalities in Petersburg were glaring.

When a house was being built, laborers carried bricks on their backs, climbing nimbly up the scaffolding, which had wooden boards instead of steps. Janitors picked up chopped wood from trestles, heaved them on their backs, and carried them up the back stairs of apartment houses. Tatar rag collectors came into the yard shouting "khalat-khalat!" Sometimes organ — grinders would come, and on one occasion I saw Petrushka, the Russian counterpart of Punch. I was somewhat taken aback by his unnaturally thin voice (the man had put a device in his mouth to alter the sound of his voice). A screen hid him from the waist up.

We went to see the hundred-year-old grenadiers from the Golden Company who stood guard at the monument to Tsar Nicholas I, whom they had served. The survivors had been brought from all over Russia to the capital.

Petersburg was a city of dark beauty hidden inside its palaces and behind the advertisements. The Winter Palace was dark at night; the tsar and his family lived in the Alexander Palace in Tsarskoye Selo. At night the cheerful rococo lost its gaiety and became heavy and gloomy. Opposite the palace, the Peter and Paul Fortress was also shrouded in darkness. The cathedral's soaring spire looked threatening like a sword out of its sheath.

The canals weaving their ways through the regular pattern of the streets upset the city's stately orderliness. The Alexandrovsky Public Gardens opposite the Admiralty offered amusements for children (rides on deer sleds in winter, a zoo and ponds with goldfish in summer), while the surrounding palaces looked on like governesses. The slightest gust of wind drove dust across the Field of Mars, and the Mikhailovsky Castle seemed to wink at you since one of its windows was bricked up. It was the window of the room where Emperor Paul had been strangled.

Time does not entirely stifle our early impressions. Sometimes a happy incident triggers memories of the past. This happened to me when I saw these old photographs. They brought back to me the feel of the Petersburg of my childhood and somehow made it close and tangible. I hope readers will understand how I felt after they have leafed through this album.

THE RUBICON OF RUSSIAN HISTORY

This book is about a great city at the turn of the twentieth century — a city that arose from the wilderness by the sole decision of Peter the Great, Russia's first emperor, a city that became the capital of the powerful northern empire and in which the empire's historical drama came to an end in February 1917.

We say "in February" rather than "in March" because, until its demise, the Russian Empire lived according to the Old Style, or Julian, calendar. By Peter's time, the whole of Europe and America had long since switched to the Gregorian calendar, but he decreed that Russia should keep to the old calendar introduced by Julius Caesar. Thus by the twentieth century, Russia lagged behind the Western world by thirteen days, a fact that had dark, mystical significance for the superstitious and was much talked about in the fashionable salons of St. Petersburg at the turn of the century. The Julian calendar remained in use until the 1917 Revolution, and thus we refer in this book chiefly to Old Style dates.

This book is a collection of photographs that were not intended as history but that have acquired historical significance with the passage of time. The beam of light focused by the impartial lens has imprinted on photographic plates some fleeting moments of Petersburg's life, and some major and minor participants in its historical drama. The unfolding story left behind these accidental traces, which at the time seemed banal and trivial but which have since become eloquent and full of meaning. These photographs were to survive the people in them and many later generations; now they bear impartial witness to these people and their times.

Here is the last Russian tsar, the last official monarch, the supreme nobleman and landowner — "the master of the Russian land," as he described himself in filling out the first national census form in 1897.

Here is a Russian *muzhik*, clad in the splendid uniform of the Imperial Guards, or in the caftan of a Russian cabby, or in the oily overalls of a factory worker. Until 1861, a Russian *muzhik* could be bought and sold: if the buyer didn't need the serf's family, he could buy him alone, very much like Uncle Tom from the novel by Harriet Beecher Stowe. And until the nineteenth century no official inquiry was instituted even if a serf was beaten to death.

The majority of the population of the vast Russian land were serfs. There were also "government peasants," who belonged to the tsar, the Emperor of All the Russias: their lot was not much better, and the tsar could, at will, present them as gifts to noblemen whom he wanted to honor. The two Catherines, Alexander I, and Nicholas I, who sat on the throne after Peter the Great, gave tens of thousands of serfs to their friends and to generals who had distinguished themselves in battle.

Although it seems incredible that serfdom was abolished in Russia only in 1861, that same year saw the outbreak of the Civil War in the United States over the abolition of slavery, and painful memories of that war have still not "gone with the wind." The manifesto of Alexander II, who believed that "it is better to free the peasants from above before they free themselves from below," liberated them, but it gave them practically no land. The peasant had to work for decades to buy out the tiny plot that yesterday's noble owner had given him for his sustenance. But that was as much as the tsar could do for the peasant in an empire of landed gentry.

The liberation of the serfs defused the situation but did not remove the basic causes of the cataclysms that would shake the powerful empire to its very roots. At the same time Russia's industrial development picked up markedly, bringing all the economic and social contradictions and human problems to a head, creating opposing classes of workers and bourgeoisie and contributing to potentially explosive social tensions. The tectonic stresses in Russian society erupted from time to time in peasant revolts and workers' strikes and the emergence of a rash of revolutionary parties (which, of course, acted illegally, since until 1905 all political parties, even those upholding the monarchy, were outlawed).

Alexander II abolished whipping with a knout and almost all other kinds of corporal punishment, including the branding of people and beatings with rods in the army. He replaced the twenty-five-year army service introduced by his father with a sensible term of conscription, introduced the *zemstvo* (a local council, providing limited self-government in the cities and in the country), instituted trial by jury, proclaimed the presumption of innocence, and established the independence and lifelong tenure of judges. It was during Alexander's reign that the first report on the state budget was published — unheard of in the empire — and that the word *glasnost* (openness or publicity) first gained currency.

The far-sighted Alexander was contemplating another epoch-making reform: in effect he was preparing a draft constitution, something Russia had never had. It would, at long last, have paved the way for the first Russian parliament, giving the people a say in matters of government, in framing and adopting laws, thus making God-given ruler in some ways responsible to the ruled — the long-suffering Russian people. It would have amounted to the renunciation of the medieval doctrine of autocracy; the tsar would have ceased to be answerable only to God and to his own conscience. But it was too late: the time for reform had run out, and processes that had begun much earlier were not amenable to the tsar's will; they proceeded with the inexorable logic of history. On March 13 (1 o.s.), 1881, the day he signed a decree convening the national assembly of *zemstvo*, Alexander II, who had survived several attempts on his life, was assassinated on the bank of the Ekaterininsky Canal by members of the revolutionary People's Will group. They were convinced that they were acting on behalf of the Russian people and for their own good.

The triumphant reactionaries tried to undo as many of Alexander's reforms as they could; the dreams of a parliament were cast aside, branded as Western liberalism, which was bad for Russia, as witness the unfortunate end to which it had brought the reform-minded tsar. It was not until a quarter of a century later that the Revolution of 1905 wrested a concession from the last tsar, Nicholas II, who agreed to the creation of a truncated kind of parliament known as the Duma. The Russian Empire was entering the last, doomed turn in the spiral of its history. Alexander II's son and grandson (Alexander III and Nicholas II) were confirmed autocrats, and they enjoyed the support of all the short-sighted people who either sincerely shared, or found it convenient to share, their views. They, in fact, represented a powerful social force that managed to block badly needed historical change for a considerable length of time and thus made revolution inevitable.

Nicholas II, to give an example, had the right, on the advice of "people concerned," to commit his nation to war. In 1905 the country itself was ill prepared for war, and its army and navy were led by inept generals and admirals. The battles of the Russo-Japanese War, waged on the fields of Manchuria, in Port Arthur, and on the eastern seas, claimed the lives of hundreds of thousands of brave men who had kept their oath of allegiance to the emperor. It required the mediation of President Theodore Roosevelt to conclude the peace, which was signed in Portsmouth, New Hampshire, on September 5, 1905 (n.s.). Russia's losses amounted to 400,000 dead, wounded, sick, and prisoners of war; it may be recalled, in comparison, that in World War II the United States lost 405,000 men in the European theater and in the Pacific, while Britain's losses in all the theaters of hostilities were 375,000.

The popular anger aroused by the unjustified, meaningless, and stupidly prosecuted war precipitated the Russian Revolution of 1905. In the incipient stages of that revolution, Nicholas tried to exercise another theoretical right of the autocrat — the right to massacre his own subjects. For on Bloody Sunday, January 22 (9 o.s.), 1905, St. Petersburg workers were conducting a peaceful march. The tsar, on the advice of his government, ordered the troops to shoot at the crowd of marchers, who carried icons of Christ the Savior, portraits of Nicholas himself, and a petition containing a "humble request" to the monarch to alleviate their burdens. The Imperial Guards and the Petersburg garrison troops discharged salvos from their guns, and the Cossacks charged into the crowds with swords near Palace Square at the beginning of Nevsky Prospekt, and at the Narva Triumphal Arch. Of the 140,000 people taking part in the march, nearly 5,000 (including many women and children) were killed or wounded. Outraged by the massacre, the parliaments of France, Britain, and Germany voted for suspension of loans to the Russian government, and political parties and societies staged rallies all over Europe and America and sent cables of protest expressing sympathy for the Petersburg workers and the Russian people.

The bloodshed on that Sunday and other massacres ordered during the Revolution of 1905 and the February Revolution of 1917 and in the two last wars waged by the Empire earned the tsar the nickname of Bloody Nicholas. The bloodshed called for vengeance, and it duly came, years later, in accordance with the ruthless law recorded in the Old Testament: an eye for an eye and a tooth for a tooth.

Our narrative accompanying the historical photographs begins long before the final days of the empire, at the turn of the twentieth century. The start of the coming century was marked by the sense of the passing of an age, a watershed when one wants to look back. And nowadays, when the twentieth century is coming to an end, we have much the same feeling.

Today, as we look back on our past, we can afford to see it not only in black-and-white, but to distinguish other colors and innumerable shades. We seem at last to be mature enough to understand what physicists have known for centuries, that the color white as such does not exist in nature. Similarly, any person who has reached a certain level of maturity today understands that the fratricidal Civil War that followed the 1917 Revolution was not just a heroic and glorious saga in the people's history, but a painful historical experience, a tragedy; that millions of deserters from that war were not a disgrace to the Russian *muzhik*, but the natural behavior of men born to live and not to kill and be killed. In the same way, the destinies of individual people, with their miseries and suffering, should not be obscured by the abstract notions of social class, the state, parties, and masses.

Can the exigencies of the Revolution justify as well as explain the trials that befell the family of Nicholas II, Empress Alexandra Feodorovna, their daughters, and their little son in their last days and hours? (They saw their own children being shot before sharing their gruesome fate.) Putting one's hand on one's heart, the answer is a firm "No." For all his mediocrity and narrow-mindedness, Nicholas II, who bears much of the blame for the actual collapse of the Russian Empire, played a contradictory role in all these events. A doting father and, incidentally, an enthusiastic photographer, a very pious person with a bent for mysticism, he welcomed the pogroms staged by the Black Hundreds and approved of brutal reprisals. He had the bad luck to have been born to the throne in a state that demanded very different qualities of its ruler, in a time that demanded

a much greater vision and personal strength. His inability to govern the country when revolutionary change was necessary inevitably led to a cruelty that seemed alien to his nature, forcing upon him a series of fateful decisions that were traditional for a Russian monarch, but irrational for his time. Yet, for all its inconsistency, "government power believed that the most convenient thing for it was to keep three-quarters of the population in the position not of people who were equal citizens, but in the position of grown-up children (creatures of a special kind)." So wrote Count Sergei Witte, who had tried to save the empire by creating the Duma and implementing liberal reforms, which earned him the reputation of a "red" at the tsar's court and the hatred of the tsar himself, who sacked him as soon as he had the opportunity. "If the government assumed a role that extended beyond the sphere of government in modern states, the role of policing, then sooner or later that government had to reap the benefits of such a regime," Witte also wrote. As is clear from his correspondence with Alexandra Feodorovna, Nicholas II believed that it was his sacred duty to safeguard Russian autocracy and hand it over intact as the family legacy of the Romanovs to his son, Alexei. For all this, he suffered retribution, but he bore it with dignity.

Today, having lived through the pathos of revolutionary struggle and unquestioning worship of allegedly inexorable and inhuman laws of the historical Moloch, and having lived through terrible, but far from inevitable tragedies and human sacrifices of the 1920s–50s, we have become keenly aware of the need for more humanism and charity. We have arrived at a more humane and less primitive view of our history and of our human and civic right and duty to take a calm and impartial view of the past.

The photographs taken at the turn of the century show familiar and unfamiliar faces, streets, and buildings that hold a fascination for us not only because these photographs are a hundred years old but, even more important, because the tensions that would lead to so many world upheavals were so clearly present in St. Petersburg then. The urge to feel its atmosphere rivets us to these old photographs, which show the face of an almost unfamiliar city, the main protagonist of Russian history over the past centuries — a city that would soon lose most of its indigenous inhabitants, many of its buildings and architectural ensembles, its original place names, and even the name with which it was christened.

Beginning in the second half of the nineteenth century, Petersburg, whose look in the first century and a half of its history is known to us only from paintings and drawings, was immortalized in tens of thousands of photographs, too many of which, like their makers or owners, have not survived the troubles of our stormy century. As camera reporting became widespread, the ubiquitous cameramen managed to take many snapshots of street life. They bear witness to major historical events, record scenes of daily life, and offer vivid portraits of people. Petersburg emerges from these photographs in all its diversity, its metropolitan splendor, and its poverty: the Imperial Family on an outing, dinners at expensive and luxurious salons and restaurants, queues for cheap meals at soup kitchens, filthy flophouses with their glum inhabitants, and the toil of the citizens.

The history of the Russian Empire's northern capital — which, beginning in the second half of the nineteenth century, was one of the world's main cultural centers and was gradually becoming the center of the revolutionary movement — cannot fail to arouse interest and invite close attention on the part of anyone who wants to understand Russia's past, with its base and noble aspects, its moments of glory and shame. As the Russian historian Vasily Kliuchevsky has said, the history of a country and its people is like the past of an individual: without knowing an individual's biography, it is impossible to understand what that individual is capable of and what he can do in the future. A documentary biography of Petersburg has much to tell us. Meetings of top government officials, bustling trade, the interpenetration of cultures, and numerous personal and family ties linked St. Petersburg by a thousand threads to the states of the Old and the New Worlds. As it matured, the city became more and more integrated into world civilization.

Before the Revolution: St. Petersburg in Photographs spans the period from 1890 to 1914, the year World War I began. It opens with the chapter "The City on the Neva" — one of its largest sections — containing photographs of street scenes, panoramas of streets, squares, and embank-ments, and pictures of individual buildings, many of which have not survived or have changed beyond recognition.

The next chapter, "Pages of History," presents diverse historical events: the celebration of St. Petersburg's bicentennial, episodes related to the Russo-Japanese War, the Revolution of 1905, the three-hundredth anniversary of the Romanov dynasty, the mobilization for World War I, and so on.

The chapter "Capital of the Empire" reflects the structure of government power, with Emperor Nicholas II at the top of the pyramid. It shows official Petersburg, the tsar's bureaucrats, visits by European heads of governments.

The chapter "It Could Be Any Day" covers every aspect of the daily life of St. Petersburg, featuring the bustling bazaars, the insides of factories, the quiet reception wards, and surgical theaters in a city hospital, the smooth efficiency of banks.

In the chapter "Cab, Tram, and Motorcar," which traces the history of city transport, are seen the early motorists and the numerous transportation workers — the carters, the cabbies, the water carriers, the rubbish collectors, and the tram drivers.

Reflected in the chapter "From Alpha to Omega" is the Russian capital as a major center of education and science, seat of the Academy of Sciences and St. Petersburg University, as well as scores of higher and secondary schools, military and religious academies, elementary schools, grammar schools, gymnasia, and commercial schools.

The book ends with glimpses of the cultural pursuits and leisure activities of St. Petersburgers, which, of course, can only begin to do justice to the galaxy of brilliant writers, poets, artists, musicians, and stage personalities whose lives were inextricably linked with Petersburg.

Many photographs have never been published before. All have been reproduced from authentic black-and-white glass-plate negatives made available by the Central State Archive of Cinema and Photo Documents in Leningrad, one of the biggest archives of its kind in the USSR.

The City on the Neva

The Neva and the Nikolayevskaya Embankment. 1910–12

Nevsky Prospekt near Gostiny Dvor. 1900

Znamenskaya Square, Nikolayevsky Station, and the
monument to Alexander III (now dismantled). 1910—12

THE CITY ON THE NEVA

Красуйся, град Петров, и стой
Неколебимо, как Россия!
Flaunt your beauty, Peter's City,
and stand unshakeable like Russia!

Alexander Pushkin
(translated by D. M. Thomas)

These two lines from Pushkin were quoted in Russian — much to the amazement of all those present — by General de Gaulle at the end of his speech in Leningrad in 1967. The French president, a Parisian who must have seen some of the most famous and magnificent cities of the world, was not given to "polite" flattery and, as a patriot of France to which he devoted his life, was anything but lavish in his praise of other countries and cities.

The immortal Russian poet Alexander Pushkin glorified the city in his poem *The Bronze Horseman*, which had as an alternative title, *Petersburg Story*. The two lines that General de Gaulle delivered in Russian provide a motto that could still be emblazoned on the city's coat of arms.

Fiodor Dostoyevsky, on the other hand, sometimes seemed almost to hate Petersburg: a gray, dull, dreary city, a phantasmagoria, a bad dream. These were the words he used to try to justify his hostile attitude to the cruel city, the capital of the empire where his "poor folk" were suffering and "the insulted and injured" were dying, and through whose streets he was himself driven to the scaffold in December 1849.

He was taken to the Semionovsky Parade Ground and, together with twenty fellow members of the "Petrashevsky Circle," they stood on the scaffold for half an hour as a sentence condemning them to death by firing squad was read out.

They were stunned by the severity of the sentence. A priest offered to hear their last confession, but only Timakovsky approached him. When the priest walked past the death row with a cross, everyone kissed it in the spirit of the Christian and utopian socialism in which they believed, a belief that had earned them the death sentence — most of them considered Jesus Christ to be a champion of the equality and fraternity of man. Dostoyevsky, speaking somewhat oddly in French, said to his friend Speshnev, "We shall be with Christ." "We shall be a handful of dust," replied the latter with a wry smile. Shrouds were put on the first three victims and they were tied to posts next to the scaffold. Beneath them were deep, gaping graves into which the bodies of all the executed were to lie. Dostoyevsky was apparently in the second group of three. At the officer's command, sixteen soldiers with loaded rifles lined up and took aim as the drums beat mutely. Then, a messenger from the Winter Palace arrived unexpectedly on horseback: the grim, sadistic show was crowned by the tsar's "pardon." The scenario was known to the executioners, but not to the victims. Nicholas I, the father of Alexander II, announced an act of mercy: the death sentence was commuted to penal servitude for most of them. This episode in Dostoyevsky's life is believed to have inspired the famous story of Prince Myshkin about the experiences of a person sentenced to death in his novel *The Idiot*. Could it be that the show of 1849 influenced the great writer's whole attitude to the city on the Neva?

"Wet granite under your feet, tall, black, grimy houses on either side of you, fog under your feet and fog over your head too," adds Dostoyevsky to his unflattering description of Petersburg. But he did not always feel that way. Elsewhere he declares his love for the city. Like everyone, anyone, Russian or foreign, who knew the seamy side of the first capital of the autocratic empire, he had a love-hate relationship with it.

A tsarist dream come true, it is a city worthy of a Roman emperor, of Julius Caesar himself — indeed, the Russian word "tsar" derives from "caesar." A fantasy city, it sprang up and grew inexorably by the whim of Peter in a place that seemed unsuited for human habitation. Low marshy banks and the wet and unwholesome climate brought untold diseases to its inhabitants and caused the deaths of thousands upon thousands of the people who were conscripted to build it. Nature took its revenge on the bold monarch who ordered the city to be built contrary to the alleged warnings of local fishermen who knew what nasty tricks the waters of the river and the sea could play. Peter I caught cold during the flood that hit his beloved city in 1724 and died, still full of vigor and brimming with ideas. Nature punished all the succeeding generations of people who were born and reared on these shores, exacting, almost yearly, a heavy toll in lives, goods, buildings, bridges, and ships. Cyclones over the Baltic, usually in autumn, cause a local rise in pressure, and because of the geographical position of the eastern part of the Gulf of Finland and the Neva Delta, a long incoming wave blocks the water in the Neva, causing much flooding. There have been three hundred floods in the city's history, with sixty floods topping the 2-meter mark and the most powerful ones reaching as high as 4 meters.

The place Peter I chose for building a city is comparatively young by the geological clock, in which a millennium is but an instant, and even by the historical clock. The last icing, which brought a 1,000-meter-thick layer of ice to the site of the future city, came about ten to twenty thousand years ago. The masses of water formed a vast sea and flooded the territory of modern Leningrad. At this time, the ancient Oriental civilizations were erecting grandiose irrigation structures in the valleys of the Nile, Tigris, and Euphrates, but here in the far north, nature was still in the throes of titanic labor. About four thousand years ago a strait 8 to 21 kilometers wide linked Lake Ladoga and the Baltic Sea. That strait would later become the valley of the Neva River. The Neva itself is young, having acquired its present shape at approximately the time of Alexander the Great. Petersburg, situated on 147 islands of the Neva Delta as of 1820 (nobody seems to know their exact number now!) is justly called "a northern Venice." The city had to struggle for every inch of dry ground. The early buildings on the swampy banks of the Neva rested on mighty wooden piles. The foundation of every embankment, street, lane, and house is filled and paved with rubble and rock brought from afar. Tsar Peter issued a decree whereby anyone arriving in the city had to pay a "stone" tax. Since then most of the city has been elevated by 2 meters and in some places by 5 to 12 meters.

Petersburg, which owed its birth to Russia's need for access to the sea — something it didn't have at the beginning of the eighteenth century — became a "window on Europe," a military outpost on a waterway leading to the West, a shipyard, and a port. It became Russia's capital in 1712, nine years after its birth.

The bleak Baltic, the northern antipode of the sunny Adriatic and Mediterranean, affected not only the look of the city, but the faces and the disposition of its citizens. In the early twentieth century, according to statistics, there were 158 days with rain and/or snow and only 35 cloudless days. An umbrella, raincoat, and galoshes are as much attributes of daily life for a Petersburger as for a Londoner. The fickle weather is the source of constant colds, complaints, jokes, and anecdotes.

But the sea was in many ways a boon. Shipbuilding and trade with Europe provided a livelihood for the city's inhabitants. From the beginning of the eighteenth century western winds brought to Russia German, English, and Dutch engineers, builders, craftsmen, merchants, and entrepreneurs, as well as Russians who had studied at the world's best universities and vast numbers of impoverished but energetic fortune seekers. Those winds also brought the latest scientific ideas, the "free thought" of the Enlightenment and socialism, and fashions from London and Paris: the window flung open by Peter exposed Russia to European life.

The sea provided protection in times of war. The Kronstadt Fortress on the island of Kotlin and other coastal fortifications blocked the approaches to the city from the West. Not once has an enemy navy been able to reach the city.

The sea naturally features prominently in the city's symbols. Petersburg's coat of arms is two crossed anchors. The Admiralty spire is topped by a light, swift sailboat, an emblem known to the whole world. The decorative Rostral Columns — the beacons celebrating Russia's naval victories — adorn the tip of Vasilyevsky Island. The numerous bas-reliefs, individual structures, and ensembles inspired by the sea show Neptune, various patron deities of local rivers, and other mythological characters associated with water and the sea.

Part of the ancient trade route from the Baltic to Greece, the Neva was a busy waterway by the late nineteenth century, a fact that was particularly noticeable inside the city. It became still busier with the building of the deep 32-kilometer Morskoi (Maritime) Canal in the Gulf of Finland, capable of accommodating ocean-going liners, the use of new, sophisticated equipment in the Petersburg port, and the reconstruction of the vast Mariinsky hydro-engineering project, which linked the Baltic to Russia's northern and southern seas. All the branches and canals were filled with innumerable wooden barges, sailboats, and tugs, ships of all shapes and sizes, Finnish *laibas* , and the ubiquitous rowboats. Petersburg would have been a different place without the rowboats and without the bridges, large and small. The number of bridges varied with time. At present there are more than three hundred, of which twenty-two are drawbridges.

Other places on the same latitude (60°) are veritable kingdoms of snow and ice — Chukotka, Alaska, Greenland. Petersburg, the northernmost of the largest cities of the world (it has a population of about four million), lies only 6° south of the Arctic Circle, which lends it a special flavor. It is true that winter here lasts five long months, but its magnificent "white nights" have always attracted dreamers, poets, and travelers.

Usually cities sprang up spontaneously and naturally, wherever suitable conditions arose. Not so Petersburg. It owed its fate to a combination of an inspired vision and sober calculations: wide, straight streets and avenues, the classically laid-out gardens and parks, neat rows mostly of stone buildings in the center. It had more sumptuous mansions and magnificent and diverse Orthodox and non-Orthodox shrines than any other Russian city, and its skyline was higher. Petersburg was unlike most European cities, despite the fact that it was designed by architects who came to Russia from many lands to win fame in their adopted country. Among them were Bartholomeo Rastrelli, who designed the Winter Palace and the Smolny Convent; Carlo Rossi, who designed the General Staff building and the Mikhailovsky Palace (now the Russian Museum); Auguste de Montferrand, who immortalized himself by building St. Isaac's Cathedral; Giacomo Quarenghi, who built the Academy of Sciences; and Antonio Rinaldi and Charles Cameron, to mention just a few. They brought their expertise, intuition, and training. They did not attempt to copy famous Western buildings but assimilated the national cultural tradition and worked side by side with Russian masters (Adrian Zakharov, Yury Velten, Andrei Voronikhin, Vasily Stasov, Andrei Starov, and others) to create the unique skyline of the northern Palmyra. The availability of vast space and huge subsidies from the tsarist treasury gave colossal scope for creative imagination and energy, which materialized on an unprecedented scale. Architectural ensembles that attempted to relate to the landscape and the surrounding buildings sprang up one after another.

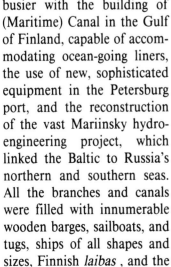

The Fontanka near Kolomna. Kalinkin Bridge. 1900s
In the background is one of the seven tower bridges that span the Fontanka. Only one of them, the Chernyshov (now Lomonosov) Bridge, has survived.

Petersburg was constantly under construction. As photographs attest, some parts of the city often changed beyond recognition within a decade. This was not surprising in a constantly growing city. However, in later periods its face sometimes changed even more dramatically and in a still shorter time. The period of the Civil War was one such time: houses were left unattended after the abolition of private ownership of real estate, and the transportation and fuel crisis led to some of the wooden structures being used for firewood by the greatly reduced population.

During World War II, the city was under siege for 900 days. On 611 of these days it was bombarded: the Nazi artillery and air force fired 150,000 shells and dropped 107,000 bombs on residential areas. The city lost 3,000 dwellings, and 7,000 buildings and 200 historical and architectural monuments suffered heavy damage. But from the times of Josef Stalin there is still a cruel uncertainty about the actual number of people who died during this time: a million more or less.

Another circumstance contributed to the city's modern look. The hatred for the tsarist regime was such that after the Revolution of 1917 massive destruction was visited on the trappings of the autocracy. Double-headed Russian eagles disappeared from the façades of buildings and grilles, from the moldings and decor of palace interiors. Many monuments, especially those of members of the Romanov dynasty, were taken off their pedestals to be replaced by hastily made gypsum figures of new heroes. As a result of the policy of restricting religious institutions, many buildings and churches became derelict and were often destroyed. The process, which began with a vengeance in the late 1920s and early 1930s, continued, albeit on a smaller scale, into the 1960s.

Finally, a massive housing development program in the late 1950s created entire new neighborhoods and increased the city's area many times over, even though the standard drab architecture hardly added to the city's beauty.

Even so, historical Petersburg can be readily seen in this new city thanks to the branches of the Neva River, the bridges, and the monumental architectural ensembles that have weathered all the storms and that lend the city a magnificently austere beauty, which has inspired poets for centuries. Its features can be spotted everywhere, sometimes in a most unexpected way: elaborate decor on gates, a disused fountain in a cozy square, stone lions

and griffons, thousands of chimney stacks, an occasional fire-watch tower, fancy bas-reliefs on some buildings, pilasters, antique figures, and monograms.

Closer to the center, signs of old Petersburg abound. The radial layout of streets and avenues, the outlines of buildings and façades, belong to old Petersburg. Only the sounds, colors, and smells are different. There is more light in the city due to the brighter colors of the walls and the evening lights. But as of old, Nevsky Prospekt is the main thoroughfare, only now it is more crowded and congested with traffic. Step off the Prospekt and you will find yourself in narrow streets with courtyards and ill-lit stairways in gray houses where Dostoyevsky's characters led a cramped existence. As of old, the Summer Garden is a favorite haunt, though some of the giant trees that Pushkin and his Onegin knew are no longer there.

The heart of Petersburg, however, its essence and character, is in the center. It is in the placid sweep of the Neva and the hub of the city. It is in the Peter and Paul Fortress, where as it has for centuries, the boom of a cannon fired from the Naryshkin bastion at noon and the chimes of the clock reverberate over the Neva and the whole city. Here the Neva splits into two wide branches to form the irregular strip of the Vasilyevsky Island, the Strelka. Its shape was followed by Thomas de Thomon in his classical ensemble of the Stock Exchange, the Rostral Columns, and the embankment. Nearby, fronting the Neva, is the Kunstkammer, Petersburg's first museum and the brainchild of the inquisitive Peter. It stands cheek-by-jowl with the focus of Russian thought, the Academy of Sciences and the University, which was housed in the Twelve Colleges, one of the earliest structures built by the great Domenico Trezzini. He devoted thirty years of his life to Petersburg. His other immortal creations include Peter I's Summer Palace, the Cathedral of Saints Peter and Paul, and the monolith of the Petersburg Fortress. Across the river from the University Embankment, on an open space in front of St. Isaac's, whose golden dome can be seen tens of kilometers away on clear days, stands the equestrian statue of the city's founder, Peter the Great, the Bronze Horseman on a rearing horse. To the right is the former Admiralty Shipyard built from Peter's own drawings eighteen months after the founding of the Peter and Paul Fortress. The circle is completed by the magnificent Winter Palace, whose whole history is linked with the old regime. The beginning and the end of the old city, the fortress-cum-prison and the palace of the tsars facing each other across the Neva, shared the same fate. They are now public museums, whose fame has transcended national boundaries.

The image of the historic city lingers in our consciousness from childhood like a beautiful melody or a perfect canvas. From any point of the circle drawn along the banks of the Neva one gets a splendid view of architectural masterpieces that look so different at different times of the day or year. The sea breeze, the sweep of the Neva River, its rough surface all bring a remarkable sense of freedom and life. Those born on the banks of the Neva are imbued with the harmony of water, stone, and air, and they find it hard to adjust themselves to the atmosphere of other cities, which to them look cramped, dreary, and somehow wanting.

Petrovskaya (Peter) Square. 1890–1900

It was originally a square fronting a bridge. Since 1727 it has been linked with Vasilyevsky Island by the Isaac floating bridge, which took its name from the nearby Cathedral of St. Isaac of Dalmatia that was first built in 1710. From the middle of the eighteenth century the square was called the Senatskaya (Senate) Square because the Senate moved there from its former building, Twelve Colleges. In 1782 it was renamed Petrovskaya Square to mark the unveiling of the first monument to Petersburg's founder, the Bronze Horseman, commissioned by Empress Catherine II. The statue, witness to the skill of the French sculptor Etienne Falconet, captures the essence of Peter I's reforms. The horseman is charging up a rock, a 1,600-ton granite monolith dubbed "thunder rock." It was carried on a specially built ship from Konnaya Lahta, on the outskirts of Petersburg. A medal commemorating that feat of transportation bore the caption: "To derring-do." It was in this square that several regiments of the Guards (about three thousand men) led by rebellious nobleman-officers refused to pledge allegiance to the new emperor Nicholas I on December 26 (14 o.s.), 1825. They tried to force his abdication and thus democratize the state and abolish serfdom. As Alexander Herzen put it, the grape-shots fired at the rebels hit the monument to Peter, the reformer of Russia. The conspirators were cruelly punished by Nicholas I. Five of them were hanged, though capital punishment had been abolished in Russia back in 1754, and the others were sent into exile and penal servitude. They became known as the Decembrists. The square was renamed Dekabristov (Decembrists) Square on the one hundredth anniversary of the uprising.

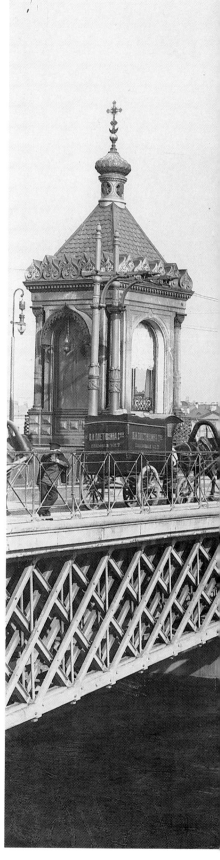

The Dvortsovaya (Palace) Embankment and a floating bridge. 1901–02

For the first quarter of a century Petersburg had no bridges, and people crossed the Neva by boat and, in winter, over ice. The first floating bridge was built in 1727. The bridges were dismantled before the Neva froze and reinstalled in the spring after the ice from Lake Ladoga had passed. They rested on rows of barges. Each of the bridges across the Neva had a draw mechanism, permitting ships to pass.

The Nikolayevsky Bridge. 1903

The first permanent wrought-iron bridge across the Neva, it incorporated state-of-the-art engineering and technology. It was opened on December 4 (November 21 o.s.), 1850, before a crowd of fifty thousand. Initially it was called the Blagoveshchensky, or Annunciation, Bridge, but in 1855 it was renamed the Nikolayevsky Bridge in honor of Emperor Nicholas I. In 1918 it was again renamed, this time after Lieutenant Piotr Petrovich Schmidt, leader of a hopeless but noble mutiny aboard the cruiser *Ochakov* in 1906. In his final statement before the military tribunal on the eve of his execution he said: "The post where I will stand to face my death will mark the boundary between two epochs in the history of my country."

The Annunciation Church of Our Lady (has not survived). Blagoveshchenskaya (Annunciation) Square. 1913

The Cathedral of Saints Peter and Paul. 1900

The Peter and Paul Cathedral, intended to be the main cathedral in the new capital, is of the same age as the Peter and Paul Fortress. The ground for the original church on the site, the wooden Church of the Apostles Peter and Paul, was broken on July 10 (June 29 o.s.), 1703. The highest structure in the city (122.5 m), the cathedral was at the same time a lightning rod for the fortress and nearby buildings, and it was indeed struck by lightning many times. The symbol of Russia's triumph on the banks of the Neva, it was a showcase for the trophies of the empire's military glory — banners captured from enemies and keys to conquered cities and fortresses. All the Russian emperors from Peter I to Alexander III and many grand dukes are buried in the cathedral.

Peter and Paul Fortress and the Neva River. 1900

The fortress, which blocked the entrance to the Neva from the Gulf of Finland and from which the city spread out, was built from Peter's own sketch. In accordance with the rules of fortification, it replicated the natural outlines of the island. Though built in great haste, it was an excellent piece of engineering in its day. For the first time in Russia, bastions were used, which made it virtually impregnable. From 1706 and over the following three decades, earthen walls were gradually replaced by stone and brick walls 10 to 12 meters high and up to 20 meters thick. More fortifications were added. The fortress never saw military action.

The Palace Embankment. The Winter Palace. 1903–04

The Winter Palace, whose architecture determined the look of the city center,
was built, according to its architect Bartholomeo Rastrelli, "solely for the glory
of all Russia." The vast building stretches along the embankment and can only
be seen in full from the opposite bank of the Neva. Splendid as its exterior may
be, its magnificent and solemn interior is even more striking. The palace was
the tsar's residence for a century and a half until the Revolution of February
1917, when it became the seat of the Provisional Government, until its fall on
November 7 (October 25 o.s.).

PRECEDING PAGES:

Mariinskaya Square and the Cathedral of St. Isaac of Dalmatia. 1900s

St. Isaac's Cathedral (May 30, according to the Church calendar, the day of St. Isaac of Dalmatia, was also Peter I's birthday). The monumental building by architect Auguste de Montferrand can be seen from a great distance. The biggest of Petersburg's cathedrals, it could hold more than 12,000 people. Some 24,000 piles supported its foundation. Girding the cathedral are 112 granite monoliths brought from near Vyborg — 48 of them are 17 meters high and weigh 114 tons each. Montferrand died in June 1858, a month after the cathedral was opened. His last wish to be buried in the cathedral was not granted by the emperor. Instead his coffin was carried around the cathedral and, after a funeral mass at St. Catherine's Roman Catholic Church on Nevsky Prospekt, was sent to Paris, where the architect was finally buried.

The Cathedral of Our Lady of Kazan. Nevsky Prospekt. 1900s

Looking at the perfect outline of this structure, it is hard to imagine that the cathedral, which was built in 1801–11 as the city's main church, has remained unfinished. According to the plan, a colonnade similar to that facing Nevsky Prospekt was to be built on its southern side. The cathedral is the burial place of Field Marshal Mikhail Kutuzov, Prince of Smolensk, the commander in chief of the Russian Army who repelled Napoleon's invasion in 1812.

The Summer Garden. 1900s

A year after the city was founded, Peter I decided to build a summer residence on the former site of a Swedish nobleman's estate. The new park and garden, which the tsar called *ogorod* (kitchen-garden), became the center of political life and court celebrations. The Summer Garden, occupying an area of some 12 hectares, had 50 fountains, none of which has survived. As late as the end of the nineteenth century, access to the park was prohibited to "dogs and lower ranks," in General Ignatyev's words.

ABOVE:

The grille of the Summer Garden and the Alexander Nevsky Chapel (has not survived). 1900

In memory of Alexander II's survival of an assassination attempt (Dmitry Karakozov fired at him in April 1866), a chapel was erected in this place with the inscription: "Do not touch the annointed sovereign." The eighth attempt on the emperor's life, which was carried out by the People's Will revolutionaries in 1881, was successful.

OPPOSITE, ABOVE:

St. Catherine's Roman Catholic Church. 32–34 Nevsky Prospekt. 1902

OPPOSITE, BELOW:

Featherbed Stalls (only Luigi Rusca's portico has survived). 33a Nevsky Prospekt. 1898

The six-column portico served as an entrance to the Featherbed Stalls, which, among other goods, offered feathers and down. Until the mid-nineteenth century, they were commonly referred to as the Women's Stalls because most of the merchants there were women.

Building of the Duma and the Chapel of the Vernicle (has not survived). 31 Nevsky Prospekt. 1900s

In 1860–61, a century after the start of the building of Gostiny Dvor, a chapel was built in front of the Featherbed Stalls with money donated by merchants. The Russian-Byzantine–style chapel was very popular among the common people.

43

The Panteleimonovsky chain bridge across the Fontanka. 1904
The first suspension bridge in Russia was dismantled in 1907 and replaced by
another bridge after a similar bridge, the Egyptian, collapsed in January 1905,
when a cavalry squadron was crossing it.

ABOVE:

**The Fontanka River with a view of the Mikhailovsky Castle.
1909—12**
The Mikhailovsky Castle was the residence of Emperor Paul I, who had accept-
ed the title of the Great Grandmaster of the Order of the Maltese Cross. It was
built as a fortress with a moat and a drawbridge in front of the main entrance.
But neither the walls nor the moat could save the monarch, who was murdered
by officers of the Guards and disgruntled noblemen on the night of March 23
(11 o.s.), 1801, only forty days after he had taken up residence there. In reply to
an offer to abdicate, he said to his assassins, "You can kill me, but I will die
your emperor!" The building was vacant until 1819, when it became the headquarters of the Main Engineering School, of which the great Russian writer
Fiodor Dostoyevsky was a graduate.

The Fontanka River. 1906

The Fontanka Embankment and the Resurrection Church (has not survived). 1900

After a huge fire at Apraksin Dvor in 1862, its owner, Count Apraksin, vowed to build a church next to the restored bazaar. The church was built between 1884 and 1887.

St. Mironius' Church (has not survived) on the Obvodny Canal. 1900s

The church was built in 1849–55 for the Life Guards of the Regiment of Chasseurs.

The German Reformed Church (partially survived).
60 Bolshaya Morskaya Street. 1910–13

**The Trinity Cathedral of the
Alexander Nevsky Abbey.
1900s**

In 1710 Peter I founded a monastery to commemorate the victory in 1240 of the Novgorod Prince Alexander (later canonized as St. Alexander Nevsky) over the Swedes on the bank of the Neva. It became the site of a religious school (from 1797) and the famous Necropolis. There lie many of the greatest men of Russia — Lomonosov, Suvorov, Voronikhin, Musorgsky, Tchaikovsky, Dostoyevsky, and others.

The Resurrection Smolny Cathedral. Ekaterininskaya (Catherine) Square. 1900s

When Quarenghi passed what the artist Alexander Benois described as one of the most beautiful and poetic edifices in Russia — the Resurrection Cathedral by Bartholomeo Rastrelli — the great architect would tip his hat as a token of respect. The elegant lines of the five-domed cathedral and the structures that surround it belie the fact that the ensemble has never been completed. According to the architect's plan, it was to be fronted by a bell tower reminiscent in outline of the Bell Tower of Ivan the Great in Moscow. The Smolny Convent was founded by decree of Elizabeth Petrovna, eldest daughter of Peter the Great. The convent was built on the site of the Smolny Yard, situated near the crownwork in the former Nyenskans Fortress, which held stocks of tar used in ship building, hence the name, Smolny (or "tar"). The building never became a true convent. It housed exclusive schools for daughters of the nobility (the Smolny Institute) and of the urban middle class (the Alexandrovsky Institute), as well as a clinic and a home for widows.

The Trinity Cathedral and the Glory Column (has not survived). Izmailovsky Prospekt. 1910

The magnificent monument, the Glory Column, unveiled on October 23 (11 o.s.), 1889, commemorated the valor of the officers and men of the Izmailovsky Regiment of the Life Guards in the Russo–Turkish War of 1877–78. A Corinthian colum built from 140 guns seized from the enemy was crowned with the statue of Glory. On the sides of the granite pedestal were episodes from the battles in which the Izmailovsky Regiment had distinguished itself.

ABOVE:

Opening of the monument to Grand Duke Nikolai Nikolayevich (has not survived). Manezhnaya (Manège) Square . 1914

The monument to Grand Duke Nikolai Nikolayevich Sr., Field Marshal and commander of the Russian Army in the Russo–Turkish War, was opened on January 24 (11 o.s.), 1914, in the presence of delegations from the Balkan countries.

Opening of the monument to army engineers in front of the Church of Saints Cosmas and Damian (have not survived). Corner of Voskresensky Prospekt and Kirochnaya Street. 1899

This was the official church of the Sapper Battalion of the Life Guards. It featured banners and plaques with the names of officers who had died in action.

The Transfiguration Cathedral of the Life Guards. Spaso-Preobrazhenskaya Square. 1900s

The fence around the cathedral was erected in 1829–32 from weapons captured from the Turks in a recent war. General Skobelev, the hero of another Russian campaign against the Turks (1877–78), is buried at the cathedral's rear wall.

OPPOSITE:
OPPOSITE:
**Office building of the Novitsky Factory of Rubber and Metal
Stamps. 23 Sadovaya Street. 1906**

ABOVE:
**Cathedral of St. Andrew the First Called and part of the
Andreyevsky Marketplace (has not survived). Vasilyevsky
Island, corner of Bolshoi Prospekt and 6th Line. 1913**

PRECEDING PAGES:
**Residential house owned by
the Rossiya Insurance Society.
27—29 Mokhovaya Street.
1900s**

Sennoi Market (has not survived) and the Assumption Church (Our Savior-on-Sennaya) [has not survived]. Sennaya Square. 1900

The church, square, and market got their name from the fact that hay (*seno*) from surrounding villages was brought and sold there.

PRECEDING PAGES:
**The Resurrection Convent
(partially preserved).
Zabalkansky Prospekt. 1900s**

**The flood of 1903.
Vasilyevsky Island**

ABOVE:
**Bolshaya Dvorianskaya
Street. 1907**

CENTER:
Cheap flats. Early 1900s

**Residential house.
60, 5th Line, Vasilyevsky
Island. 1900s**

City's outskirt. Obvodny Canal. 1900s

ABOVE:

**Warehouses of the Evangelical Society for Religious and Moral
Instruction of Protestants. 7 Narvskaya (Narva) Square. The
Narva Triumphal Arch is seen in the background. 1913—14**

OPPOSITE:

The Narva Triumphal Arch. 1900s

Pages of History

Celebrations of the three-hundredth anniversary of the Romanov dynasty. People's House of Emperor Nicholas II. 1913

Procession in Peter I Square celebrating the bicentenary of St. Petersburg. June 9 (May 27 o.s.), 1903

A procession organized by the Alliance of the Russian People.
Nevsky Prospekt. 1907

Opening of a new bridge named after
Peter the Great across the Neva. 1911

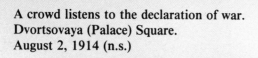

A crowd listens to the declaration of war.
Dvortsovaya (Palace) Square.
August 2, 1914 (n.s.)

PAGES OF HISTORY

Petersburg, Petrograd, Leningrad... These names span a dramatic and glorious period of almost three hundred years in the life of the city on the Neva River, the city whose destiny is linked with the major milestones of Russian history.

In 1703 the Northern War with Sweden was in its third year. Russia was seeking to regain the lands that originally belonged to the domain of Novgorod but that had been lost during the Times of Trouble: the Polish and Swedish invasion in the early seventeenth century. Peter I secured the coveted outlet to the Baltic Sea and Europe in 1702 by seizing the Swedish fortress of Nöteborg (formerly Russian Oreshek), at the mouth of the Neva, which flows out of Lake Ladoga. In April 1703 he captured the fortress of Nyenskans situated near where the Okhta River flows into the Neva. To protect the mouth of the Neva, the fortress of St. Petersburg (later the Peter and Paul Fortress) was founded on Vesioly Island on the Neva Delta on May 27 (16 o.s.), 1703. The fortress gave its name to the city that soon grew up around it. According to Christian lore, Apostle Peter is the keeper of the keys of the Kingdom of Heaven. Apparently Peter I attached symbolic significance to the name of the new city, for possession of the territory was indeed of key strategic significance.

Construction proceeded apace. Wooden and earthen walls, whose outlines are followed by the present fortress, were erected during the summer of 1703. Every year tens of thousands of people from all parts of the country were conscripted to work on the construction site. Alexei Tolstoy drew a vivid picture: "Floods washed away the works, fires devastated them; hunger and disease mowed down the builders, but more and more masons, carpenters, and tanners streamed along the muddy roads and forest paths. Some were shackled to prevent them from escaping. Others were flogged to death at the mile posts and in front of the huts of local judges; bewhiskered dragoons in green outlandish caftans had no mercy on the victims."

No fortifications could guarantee a future for the young city so long as the Swedish king, the young and daring Karl XII, was with his army near Russia's borders. Only the victory over the Swedes at Poltava in 1709, which Peter described as a "stone in the foundation of St. Petersburg," followed by the seizure of the Swedish fortress of Vyborg (150 kilometers north of the city) and the speedy construction of a fleet on the Baltic, secured the city's position, although the Northern War did not end until 1721.

In 1712 Petersburg became the capital of Russia. This opened a new page in the country's history. "It may be," wrote Alexei Tolstoy, "that the tsar cut the window [on Europe] through the very bones and flesh of the people; it is true that the meek peasants perished in the great draft that resulted without knowing who had claimed their lives and why; it may be that the tsar's actions made a crack that ran across the whole of slumbering Russia — and yet the window had been cut and fresh winds burst into the antiquated houses of the *boyars*, drove people out of warm beds and stirred them into action. They streamed toward the expanded Russian borders to pursue the common goals of the state."

As the poet Alexander Pushkin said, Russia joined the "circle of European powers like a ship launched to the knocking of the axe and the booming of guns." The burgeoning of industry, the creation of the Northern Navy and the biggest regular army in Europe, the expansion of diplomatic, cultural, and trade links, the subjugation of the Church to the state, a new capital, an alphabet, a new calendar, new schools, the Academy of Sciences, the first Russian newspaper, a new government structure — all this undermined the traditional way of life, which could not withstand the onslaught of Peter's reforms. But a heavy price was paid for the rapid transformation of the traditional tsardom of Muscovy into the great Russian Empire: the devastation of the country and dramatic worsening of the plight of the masses.

Peter's death brought on a time of trouble not unlike that in the early seventeenth century following the death of Ivan IV (the Terrible) and his immediate successors. It was marked by a fierce power struggle between various groups of the nobility, which had little to do with the interests of the people and the state. It was a period of "time servers," favorites and officers of the guard, and frequent palace coups. The last of them occurred at the end of June 1762, and it brought to the throne the wife of Peter III, who was assassinated soon after the coup d'état. She was Sophia Frederica Augusta of Anhalt-Zerbst, a German princess who is better known in history as Catherine the Great. During her thirty-four-year reign, Catherine, who thought herself to be a successor and spiritual heiress of Peter the Great, exhibited extraordinary intelligence, energy, and strength of character. More farsighted than other sovereigns, she managed to be on good terms with the French Enlightenment thinkers and, at the same time, to strengthen absolutism in Russia. Her reign represented the "golden age" of the gentry. But the privileges granted to it dealt a blow to the Russian peasant, triggering an unprecedented wave of peasant revolts and uprisings. The greatest peasant war was led by Emelyan Pugachov, a Cossack who proclaimed himself to be the dead emperor Peter III, Catherine's husband. So great was the sweep and power of the popular uprising that the empress, who was only able to breathe a sigh of relief after its leader was executed, sharply turned the political helm to the right and became still more assiduous in strengthening autocracy and serfdom.

The pace of Russia's historical clock, which seemed to be catching up with that of its European neighbors in the early years of Catherine's reign, slowed down again. The striking contrast between Europe and Russia in the early nineteenth century, which was clear to the Russian armies as they pursued Napoleon, made the progressive people of Russia feel ashamed and pained for their country. They believed that rapid change was necessary. The members of the Northern and Southern Secret Societies tried to implement Alexander I's timid and ineffectual attempts to free the serfs. They hoped to seize power in a military coup timed for the accession to the throne of the new emperor, Nicholas I. The brave action of the revolutionaries of the gentry (the "Decembrists") on December 26 (14 o.s.), 1825, when the insurgent regiments lined up in Petersburg's Senate Square hoping to force Nicholas's abdication, marked the beginning of the liberation movement in Russia.

Nicholas's reactionary regime had a crippling effect on Russia, which became manifest in every aspect of national life in the mid-nineteenth century. The country's backwardness was evident during the Crimean War of 1853–56 when Russian soldiers using outdated weapons were pitted against British and French soldiers who used the newer carbines. A declining international prestige, primitive industry, medieval agriculture with 30 million serfs, and grave social and ethnic tensions throughout the vast territory stretching from Poland to Alaska — this was the true meaning of the words Nicholas I said to his son shortly before his death: "The crew you inherit is not in full order."

Yet even the reforms carried out by his son Alexander II in the 1860s, notably the Great Reform, which at long last abolished serfdom, failed to give peasants land. The lofty notion of freedom remained to many of them an abstraction unrelated to the harsh reality of their continued peonage.

As it lurched into the twentieth century, Russia was torn by internal strife. Although the country enjoyed a relatively developed capitalism, it still lagged behind the leading capitalist countries — England, France, Germany, and the United States — in terms of the volume of industrial output and the equipment of its industry. The monopolization of certain industries and the concentration of production had reached a high level. Natural resources and cheap manpower attracted foreign investments, which accounted for as much as 50 percent in some industries. However, hangovers of the feudal Russia of serfdom were still in evidence in many areas of life. "The most backward farming, the most savage village — and the most advanced industrial and financial capitalism." This was how Lenin described the peculiar situation in Russia at the turn of the century.

The main legacy of serfdom in the country's economy was the continuing prevalence of large landed estates: thirty thousand landowners including the first among them, the tsar, owned about as much land as 10.5 million peasant households. The tsarist empire at the beginning of the twentieth century lacked elementary democratic freedoms: freedom of expression, freedom of the press, assembly, etc. Compounding the situation was the multinational population. Many large and small non-Russian nationalities accounting for 57 percent of the population and officially called "foreign-born," were subjected to brutal exploitation.

The early secret societies of "a hundred conspirators" — the future Decembrists — "the phalanx of heroes," as the writer Alexander Herzen called them, the "warriors cast from pure steel from head to toe" and the stormy events that, to use John Reed's expression, "shook the world" in 1917, were a century apart. It was a dynamic century, which saw wars and revolutions, the collapse of serfdom and the overthrow of the Romanov dynasty, which had ruled Russia for over three hundred years. It was an age that saw an upsurge of liberated social thought, which was awakened by Herzen's journal *Kolokol* (*The Bellhair*), published in exile, and which found its expression and elaboration in the writings and works of the Revolutionary Democrats, utopian Russian socialists, and the early proletarian revolutionaries. It was an age that saw on the one hand a fast-growing gulf between the universally recognized achievements of Russian science, literature, and arts, changes in social consciousness, and the burgeoning of young Russian capitalism, which opened new vistas for the country, and on the other hand the crude reality of peasant Russia hamstrung by numerous vestiges of serfdom.

Bloody Sunday. At the Winter Palace, January 22 (9 o.s.), 1905
On January 22 (9 o.s.), 1905, more than 140,000 workers, wearing their Sunday best, marched to the Winter Palace to ask the tsar to alleviate their lot. Their naive faith in their sovereign evaporated under a hail of bullets. No precise figure of the number of casualties is available, although some estimates put it as high as five thousand. People fell in twos and threes, crouched, pressing their hands to their stomachs; they ran limping, crawled, leaving bright red splotches behind in the snow.
The photograph you see here was taken several hours before the first shots were fired.

Tekhnologicheskaya (Technological) Square and the Technological Institute, where the first meeting of the Petersburg Soviet of Workers' Deputies was held in 1905
During the Revolution of 1905 the political involvement of the masses grew dramatically. Workers themselves exercised freedom of expression, assembly, and the press and introduced an eight-hour working day. It was then that the Soviets of Workers' Deputies, the bodies of revolutionary power, first sprang up in Russia. The Petersburg Soviet was born on October 30 (17 o.s.), 1905. Representatives of the factories gathered for a mass rally at the Technological Institute at about noon, and in the evening of the same day the first meeting of the Soviet of Workers' Deputies was held. The soviet represented some 200,000 Petersburg workers. Its first chairman was G. S. Khrustaliov-Nosar, a barrister, who was not a member of any party. Later he became a Menshevik. After his arrest, he was succeeded by Leon Trotsky.

In the early twentieth century, just like in the times of Gogol, this prompted a mixed feeling of pride, sadness, and wrath, inducing Russia's best people, who were increasingly aware of their responsibility for the country's destiny, to look for a way out of the impasse. Every decade brought new experience in the liberation struggle, which involved much suffering. The idea of freedom was advanced through the ideas of Nihilism and the actions of the terrorists, through the sacrifices of the Narodniki (populists who pinned their hopes on the peasant commune), through anarchic revolt, and through inevitable sacrifice and errors, and finally the renunciation of naive and futile dreams of a wise, fatherly monarch who cared for his subjects.

Russia's entry into a new and final phase of the liberation movement, which involved all social strata, was an inevitable and logical phenomenon that struck at the very heart of the vast empire. Petersburg, fenced off from the rest of Russia by impenetrable forests and fields, was unaffected by the innumerable peasant revolts that rocked the country for two centuries and that engulfed the estates and mansions of the landowners. It was bypassed by the numerous wars Russia waged on its borders and even the invasion of Napoleon, the brief ruler of Europe, during which the ancient capital of Moscow was burned down after the Battle of Borodino. But Petersburg was the scene of the last act.

Spurred by the tragic events in the Russo-Japanese War (1904–05), soaked in the blood of thousands of people shot in the streets of the capital, the Revolution of 1905 wrested from the monarchy a manifesto that granted basic freedoms and the "constitutional" acts of 1906 that led to the convening of a limited legislature — the Duma. The main parties of the Russian bourgeoisie — the Constitutional Democrats (Kadets) and the Alliance of October 17 (Octobrists), which was according to the Kadet leader, Pavel Miliukov, "His Majesty's opposition and not an opposition to His Majesty," the Socialists-Revolutionaries (SRs), whose main base was the peasantry; the Russian Social Democratic Labor Party (RSDLP), which in 1903 split into Mensheviks and Bolsheviks (led by Lenin); anarchists; and a plethora of other parties and groups — constituted the broad political spectrum of Russia.

The sumptuous and lavish celebrations held in the early decades of the twentieth century marking the bicentenary of the founding of Petersburg (1903), the jubilees of the Battles of Poltava (1909) and of Borodino (1912), the grandiose celebration of the tricentenary of the Romanov dynasty (1913), and numerous high-society balls and ceremonies initially served to obscure the fact that the foundations of autocracy were literally crumbling. But, caught up as it was in the maelstrom of European diplomacy, entangled in dynastic and court intrigues, and most importantly, incapable of coping with the basic social and economic problems of Russian society, the autocracy was heading toward its demise. World War I dotted every "i."

The photographs taken in the early days of that war show the faces of doomed people who do not yet suspect their fate: the emperor, whose declaration of war, in fact, ensured his own death sentence; loyal subjects demonstrating their patriotism in front of the Winter Palace and soon to be scattered all over the world, cursing an emperor who conceded nothing and so lost everything; young recruits embarking on a long march to the trenches and their anonymous graves — they all faced a long road leading nowhere.

The history of Petersburg was coming to an end: the story of Petrograd and, shortly, Leningrad was about to begin.

A party of political prisoners being sent from the Petersburg transit prison to exile in the Turukhansk Territory. 6 Konstantinogradskaya Street. August 15 (2 o.s.), 1906
Nicholas II ordered the creation of military courts during the Revolution of 1905 (between August 1905 and April 1906, they passed more death sentences than had been passed in the preceding eighty years). The tsar pardoned those who staged pogroms and murdered revolutionaries but was ruthless toward those who challenged the autocracy. In the first wave of reaction to hit the capital, about seven thousand people were exiled, about one thousand arrested, thirteen newspapers and magazines were closed, the work of forty-two printshops was suspended, demonstrations and rallies were banned, and many trade unions were closed. Simultaneously, the tsar issued his Manifesto of October 30 (17 o.s.), 1905, which "guaranteed" the basic civic freedoms and the establishment of a "representative" Duma.

Celebration of the bicentenary of St. Petersburg. Peter's wherry being carried out of Peter's House. 1903
Peter's boat is one of the most important relics of the Russian Navy. The inquisitive young Russian tsar used it to learn navigation on the Yauza River and on the pond in Izmailovo near Moscow. Two years after the end of the Northern War, on August 22 (11 o.s.), 1723, a grand feast took place in Kronstadt to celebrate the "grandfather of the Russian fleet."

87

Monument to Peter I (has not survived). Peterhof. 1900s

The bronze monument re-creates an episode during the tsar's visit to France in May–June 1717. Bidding farewell to seven-year-old King Louis XV, Peter I took him into his arms and, according to legend, exclaimed: "The whole of France is in my arms!"

**Monument to the "Carpenter Tsar" (has not survived).
The Admiralteiskaya (Admiralty) Embankment. 1910**

The monument is symbolic. The contradictory and controversial figure of Peter I, an impetuous and despotic monarch whose behavior often shocked contemporaries, also commanded a feeling of profound respect. Intolerant of sloth and indolence, he was the first to learn sciences and crafts, earning himself the reputation of a tireless worker.

Alexander Pushkin wrote of him, "Now an academician, now a warrior, now a sailor, now a carpenter, with an all-embracing soul, he was an eternal worker on the throne." A geographer and mathematician, builder of fortresses, and an astronomer, Peter especially excelled in ship building; fortresses and first-class ships were built from his drawings.

Monument to "Peter the Savior" (has not survived). The Admiralty Embankment. 1903

The monument shows an episode from the life of Peter I, who personally supervised the building of ships for the first Russian Navy and took part in naval voyages and battles.

Opening of a monument to Peter I (has not survived) near the Cathedral of St. Sampsonius. 1909

This monument to Peter was unveiled during the celebration of the bicentenary of the Battle of Poltava, which marked a turning point in the course of the Northern War between Russia and Sweden in 1709.

The smashed carriage of Plehve, minister of the interior, after his assassination. 1904

Minister of the Interior Viacheslav von Plehve was killed by a one-pound bomb thrown by a terrorist, the Socialist-Revolutionary (SR) Egor Sozonov on July 28 (15 o.s.), 1904. Russia was plagued by a rash of such attacks at the time.

The party's code of honor demanded that a terrorist remain after attempting to murder a government official, sentenced by the party for his "crimes against the people," to obey the policemen and to surrender his own life to the court's verdict. Egor Sozonov was gravely wounded himself in the action.

Half a century later Albert Camus, a brilliant French novelist, playwright and Nobel Prize winner, became fascinated with the outstanding personality of one such SR-terrorist of the time, Ivan Kaliayev, and wrote a play *The Just Assassins*, dedicated to his last tragic days. Since those times, however, few assassins, in Russia and elsewhere, have followed the principle of surrendering their own lives in return for the lives they took from others.

ABOVE:

Seamen welcomed after the Battle of Chemulpo.
April 29 (16 o.s.), 1904

"The New Year 1904 began fortissimo with the roar of the sudden war with Japan," recalled the artist Alexander Benois.

"It came out of the blue for us, for people in my milieu. But it appears that other circles — those 'who ought to know' — were also taken by surprise. This was the first real war into which Russia had been drawn since 1878, but initially no one thought of it as a real war." Plehve, the interior minister, thought it would be a "short, victorious war," which Russia needed in order to "contain the revolution." The expected triumph was to defuse mounting tensions in the country. But contrary to expectations, Russia suffered defeat, and the ruling circles had to make the best of it. That was why Petersburg gave such a pompous and solemn welcome to the tragically valiant seamen returning from the Far East, a welcome that might have been given by Romans to their victorious generals. They were welcoming the heroic crews of the Russian cruiser *Varangian* and the gunboat *Korean*, which were in the neutral Korean port of Chemulpo when the war broke out; the sailors scuttled their ships after an unequal battle with the Japanese squadron.

Wounded soldiers arriving from the Russo-Japanese front being sent to the Nikolayevsky military hospital.
63 Suvorovsky Prospekt. 1905

Opening of the Kolomna department of the Assembly of Russian Factory Workers in Petersburg. Georgy Gapon and Mayor-Administrator Fullon are in the center. November 1904

The "assemblies" of factory workers discussed drafts of the petition to the tsar setting out their vital needs and demands. The final draft of the petition, signed by Georgy Gapon on the night of January 20 (7 o.s.), 1905, which he intended to hand to Nicholas II, read as follows:

"Your Majesty! We, the workers and citizens of St. Petersburg, belonging to different estates, our wives, children, and helpless old parents have come to you, Your Majesty, in search of truth and protection. We are impoverished. We are being oppressed and burdened with unbearable labor, we are being maltreated, we are not recognized as people, we are treated as slaves who must endure their miserable lot and keep silent.

"We have endured, but we are being pushed still further into the abyss of poverty, disenfranchisement, and ignorance; we are being strangled by despotism and arbitrary rule, and we are choking. We cannot stand it any longer, Your Majesty. Our patience has run out."

ABOVE:

**A rally in front of the Imperial St. Petersburg University.
October 31 (18 o.s.), 1905**

**A church service organized by the Black Hundreds in connection
with the publication of the tsar's Manifesto on October 30
(17 o.s.), 1905. Sennaya Square, October 31 (18 o.s.), 1905**

From the charter of the Alliance of the Russian People:
"The interest of the country lies in the unshakable preservation of Russian autocracy, Orthodoxy, and nationality, in the establishment of the State Duma,
law, and order.
Count Sergei Witte admitted: "It was difficult to identify and draw a line between the agents of the secret police and the security department and the members of the so-called Alliance of the Russian People."

Georgy Valentinovich Plekhanov, major theoretician and propagator of Marxism. 1910s

As early as 1883, Plekhanov organized a Marxist group called "Emancipation of Labor" in Geneva. It later provided the basis for the Russian Social Democratic Labor Party.The immediate political task of the RSDLP, proclaimed in the program adopted at its Second Congress in 1903, was "the overthrow of the autocracy of the tsar and its replacement with a Democratic Republic." In late 1903 Plekhanov joined the Menshevik wing of the party, and upon his return to Russia after the February Revolution of 1917, he headed the group of Mensheviks called "Unity," who believed that Russia should defend itself in the war against Germany. He believed that Russia was not ready for socialist transformations and looked askance at the October Revolution. He did not oppose Soviet power, however.

**Vladimir Ilyich Ulyanov
(Lenin) with members of the
Petersburg "Alliance for the
Emancipation of the Working
Class." Left to right: (stand-
ing) A. L. Malchenko, P. K.
Zaporozhets, A. A. Vaneyev;
(sitting) V. V. Starkov, G. M.
Krzhizhanovsky, V.I. Ulya-
nov, L. Martov (Yu. O. Ze-
derbaum). February 26 –
March 1 (February 14–17
o.s.), 1897**

Recalling how this photograph was
taken, L. Martov wrote that on the
eve of their exile to Siberia the
"condemned members of the Alliance had taken an unprecedented
liberty which to some extent broke
the conspiratorial rules."

Deputies to the Third Duma.
1907–12

The Third Duma (November 14 [1
o.s.], 1907 – June 22 [9 o.s.], 1912)
was the only one of the four Russian Dumas that lasted for the
whole of the prescribed five-year
term. It had six deputies represent-
ing the workers, four of whom were
Bolsheviks: M. G. Poletayev (sitting, second from left), M. V. Zakharov, S. A. Voronin, P. I. Surkov.

Banquet of the members of the Constitutional Democratic Party. 1910–12

From the program of the Constitutional Democratic Party adopted by the party's first congress, held in October 1905:

"The Main Law of the Russian Empire should guarantee to all the peoples inhabiting the Empire not only full civic and political equality of all citizens, but also the right of free cultural self-determination."

As Pavel Miliukov, leader of the Kadets (CDP) wrote, "The essence of our tactics lies in directing the revolutionary movement into the channel of parliamentary struggle. For us, consolidating the habits of free political life is a means of ending, and not carrying on the revolution."

Meeting of the members of the Alliance of October 17 at the Duma. 1913

From the Appeal and program of the Alliance of October 17:
"Towering over countless private and local interests, over one-sided goals of various classes, social estates, nationalities, and parties, the monarchy under the present conditions is called upon to perform its mission — to be a pacifying element in the acute struggle, political, national, and social — for which great scope has now been given by the proclamation of political and civil freedom."

The summer cottage in Ozerki, where Georgy Gapon was executed. Standing on the porch are forensic experts. April 1906

The priest Georgy Apollonovich Gapon, who played such a dramatic role as a guiding spirit behind the procession on January 22 (9 o.s.), a complex, mentally unstable person, with a dubious reputation, was suspected of having links with the tsar's security police. Having returned from abroad, where he had escaped after Bloody Sunday, Gapon was exposed as an agent provocateur and hanged on a clothes hanger by a group of workers, his former followers, at a secluded summer cottage in Ozerki in the suburbs of Petersburg. The execution took place on April 10 (March 28 o.s.), 1906. The body was discovered by the police a month later.

The body of Georgy Gapon. Ozerki. April 1906

ABOVE:

**Terrorists attack and rob a treasury vehicle. Fonarny Lane.
October 1906**

The attack was made on October 27 (14 o.s.) shortly before noon at the corner
of Fonarny Lane and Ekaterininsky Canal. Having thrown several bombs at the
escort and under the hoofs of the horses of the carriage in which the assistant
treasurer of the port customs house was carrying over 600,000 rubles in bonds,
securities, and cash, the terrorists, firing revolvers, seized bags with valuables
worth 398,772 rubles, 24 kopecks.

The second meeting of the Council of the "maximalist" Socialists–Revolutionaries held in the last third of October 1906 passed this ruling on the question of
expropriations: "1) To endorse the decision of the First Party Congress which
allows the confiscation only of government money and weapons. Those who ex-
propriate private property are automatically expelled from the Party. 2) Any
expropriation is carried out with the permission and under the supervision of
the Regional Committee, the Regional Committee seeking to take the initiative
and organize major expropriations."

**The summer house of Piotr Stolypin after the bomb
explosion. Aptekarsky Island. August 25 (12 o.s.), 1906**

"We decided to assassinate Stolypin at any cost," said O. Klimova, who took
part in preparing the assassination. "Because we were sure that the executioners
would not be allowed into the ministry building, we prepared exceptionally
powerful charges weighing 16 pounds each, which would completely destroy the
summer house. We were, of course, aware that there could be accidental victims
because the minister was to give a reception on August 25. Although the decision to sacrifice outsiders was taken after much soul-searching, we believed it
was inevitable in view of all the consequences of Stolypin's criminal activity."
Pulling up at the minister's dacha, three members of the SRs ("maximalists")
alighted from a landau. They carried briefcases and headed for the entrance.
Spotting a false beard worn by one of them, a guard rushed toward him and
tried to snatch the briefcases away from him. At that moment all three shouted
"Long live freedom! Long live anarchy!" and dropped the briefcases in front of
them simultaneously. As a result, thirty-two people were killed, twenty-two
wounded. The terrorists died. The minister was unscathed.

A group of members of the First Duma in front of a prison gate. 5 Arsenalnaya Embankment. 1908

In July 1906 Nicholas II issued a decree disbanding the Duma after the Constitutional Democrats submitted a bill whereby landowners were to be deprived of part of their lands for a redemption fee. The deputies who disagreed with the order went to Vyborg, Finland, and issued an appeal calling on the people to "stand up" for the Duma and, pending the convocation of a people's government (that is, of a new Duma), "not to give a kopeck to the Treasury, and not to give a soldier to the army," and not to recognize government loans. The participants in the Vyborg meeting were victimized: they were dismissed from their jobs, churchmen were stripped of their holy orders, noblemen expelled from "societies of the nobility" and arrested. At a trial held on December 25–31 (12–18 o.s.), 1907, 167 out of the 169 members of the First Duma were sentenced to a three-month imprisonment.

ABOVE:

Vladimir Nabokov (right), member of the First Duma, who signed the "Vyborg Appeal," arrives to be taken to prison.

The writer Vladimir Nabokov later recalled: "In becoming one of the leaders of the Constitutionalist Democratic Party (later renamed Party of the People's Freedom), my father had contemptuously forfeited his court title. After refusing to drink the Czar's health at a certain banquet, he had cooly advertised his court uniform for sale in the newspapers.... All this was a long time ago, and several years were to pass before a certain night in 1922, at a public lecture in Berlin, when my father shielded the lecturer (his old friend Miliukov) from the bullets of two Russian Fascists and, while vigorously knocking down one of the assassins, was fatally shot by the other."

ABOVE:

Nicholas II on the balcony of the Winter Palace before announcing Russia's entry into World War I. August 2 (July 20 o.s.), 1914

In connection with the start of hostilities on the Austro-Serbian border, Nicholas II ordered a general mobilization in Russia on the evening of July 30 (17 o.s.). The Decree was published on July 31 (18 o.s.), and at midnight Germany presented Russia with an ultimatum demanding the cancelation of the mobilization. On the evening of August 1 (July 19 o.s.), 1914, Count Pourtalès, the German ambassador to Russia, called on Foreign Minister Sergei Sazonov for an answer. After receiving a negative answer, he handed in a note declaring war. The following day a manifesto announcing Russia's entry into the war was read out to the people.

Mobilized soldiers accompanied by their relatives heading for the barracks. The Field of Mars. August 1914

The people of St. Petersburg waiting for early news from the
front before newspaper offices. The corner of Nevsky Prospekt
and Sadovaya Street. August 1914

Capital of the Empire

Members of the Imperial Family on board a yacht
near the Dvortsovaya (Palace) Embankment. 1903

Review of mounted police in the Field of Mars. July 27
(14 o.s.), 1909

Raymond Poincaré, President of the French Republic, arrives in Petersburg. Left to right: Poincaré, President-Minister Viviani, Vice-Admiral Le Beri. On the deck of the admiral's battleship *France*. July 1914

CAPITAL OF THE EMPIRE

The Byzantine two-headed eagle was the emblem of the state of Muscovy and of the Russian Empire for several centuries. The Russian autocracy traced its origins to Byzantium, which in turn was a successor to Rome. This idea was expressed in the formula "Moscow is the Third Rome." The regal, predatory bird, its crowned heads facing the West and the East, symbolized an empire that stretched thousands of miles over the Eurasian continent. Ethnically a mosaic — Asian from a European point of view and European from an Asian point of view — for centuries it was torn apart by the incompatibility of the diverse cultures and traditions that it tried to assimilate.

Peter I devoted his life to transforming Russia, often acting ruthlessly and despotically. By imposing education and progress with the whip and the bayonet, he gave a new impetus to old Muscovy, which lagged behind civilized Europe. Although it had become a European power under Peter, Russia "did not join — strong and elegant — the feast of great powers," wrote Alexei Tolstoy. "Dragged by the hair, bleeding and mad with fear and despair, it presented itself to its new kin in a pitiful and unequal state — as a slave. However formidable the roar of the Russian guns, the great country was slavish and obsequious before the whole world."

The writer's words are more than a vivid metaphor. The great empire was, until its very end, a "land of slaves, a land of masters." Russian peasants, who became serfs finally and totally under the Synodic Statute of Tsar Alexei Mikhailovich, the father of Peter I, in 1649 — the year of Cromwell's victory over King Charles I in England — were not freed until 1861. By that time the last manifestations of medieval despotism were vanishing in Europe: parliamentary republics or constitutional monarchies had been established practically all over the continent. But the Russian peasant could still be traded away, exchanged, or presented as a gift, even in the middle of the nineteenth century.

Despotism, lawlessness, and a slavish mentality permeated the whole of society. The obedience, patience, and muteness that characterized the lower orders also eroded and crippled the morality of the landowners, who were, on the one hand, used to exercising an unbridled and arbitrary rule over their dependent "peasant souls," and, on the other, were themselves totally dependent of the whims and favors of the autocratic system, including, of course, those of the monarch himself. It is telling that noblemen, even those related to Peter I by blood, still had to resort to ritual formulas of self-abasement traditionally used in addressing a Moscow autocrat: "Thine low-born serf, Fedka Romodanovsky, beats his old head on the floor at Thine Feet and offers his unworthy greetings to Thou, Great Lord." So wrote Prince Fiodor Yuryevich Romodanovsky, a famous associate of Peter, one of his teachers, and the same man who held unlimited powers as the tsar's deputy in Muscovy during his journeys and military campaigns. The reforming tsar's uncle, Lev Kirillovich Naryshkin, had to address the tsar in almost the same words. As for people who were close to Peter's heirs, for all their honors and the splendor of their estate, they lived on the edge of a volcano that might warm them but might also destroy them, to which thousands of examples from Russian history attest. At the top of the imperial pyramid was the monarch, who wielded unlimited powers. He had the final say in the promulgation of laws, imposed any taxes he wished, appointed ministers and high officials, gave orders to the government, and decided single-handedly questions of war and peace. The state treasury and all the wealth of the empire were his personally, and he disposed of it as he saw fit. No Western monarch had possessed such powers since the eighteenth century. The Russian tsar had more grounds for saying "L'Etat c'est moi!" than had the Sun King himself. However, he depended on the support of big landowners and, later, of the influential bourgeoisie, and he had indeed to take their interests into account.

Even Alexander I in the early nineteenth century, though aware of the need for radical change in relations between the peasant and the landowner, did not dare to implement the liberalizing reforms he had drafted. In the final analysis everyone — from top to bottom — was the slave of the empire, a self-sufficient and powerful military-bureaucratic state. "The combined effect of despotism and freedom, education and slavery is a political squaring of the circle, a riddle we have grappled with for two centuries since the times of Peter and have not yet solved," wrote Vasily Kliuchevsky, one of the most outstanding historians of Russia in the early twentieth century.

For Russian sovereigns this was no paradox: Catherine II strove to project an image of an enlightened empress. A friend of the French Encyclopedists, she corresponded with Voltaire and invited Diderot to Russia. She made vague promises of liberal reforms and new laws hinting that in this noble undertaking she would be guided by the ideas of Montesquieu and the Enlightenment generally. The estates even began to choose deputies, and Catherine published her "mandate" to them — high-minded but couched in cautious, general terms, it remained a dead letter. Before long the great peasant uprising of Emelyan Pugachov broke out, a war against landowners and the state of serf-owners — and the government cast aside its liberal pretensions and its admiration for the Enlightenment. The uprising was crushed by regiments of the regular army, deputies of the estates never assembled, a state guided by law was never created, and Russia was "back to square one."

The Russian empress was not the only monarch of her time who toyed with the ideas of the Age of Reason and "the Spirit of Laws," — Emperor Joseph II of Austria took them up sincerely and seriously, Frederick the Great of Prussia was another temporary protector of Voltaire and was himself a writer; their reforms, too, made little progress, but there were essential differences: first, the powers of the autocracy in their countries were to a degree limited and, second, some changes did succeed.

A private conversation between Catherine II and her personal secretary, Alexander Khrapovitsky, on the role of a "real" monarch tells us more about the enlightened empress's views on the rights of the monarch than her talks with Diderot, her articles in journals, and her dramas and comedies. Catherine made an imperious gesture with her hand, "my single motion sets the direction in which everything should move."

Another august disciple of the European Enlightenment, Alexander I (Catherine II's grandson), abandoned liberal reforms, which probably would have included the abolition of serfdom, at the turn of the eighteenth century. His father, killed by conspirators — officers of the guards and noblemen — had shared the same fate as Roman "caesars". This was a constant reminder to him.

And yet the Enlightenment and the French Revolution were not entirely lost on Russia, on Europe, or the world. On December 26 (14 o.s.), 1825, intellectuals of the nobility staged a heroic uprising in Petersburg, an uprising on behalf of the Russian people, against serfdom and spiritual bondage, for a republic or at least for a constitutional monarchy. The rebels (called the Decembrists) were also officers of the guards and children of noblemen, many of them came from famous Russian families, some belonged to the Rurikovich family descended from the first legendary dynasty of the rulers of Old Rus. The motives for their revolt were entirely intellectual and were at odds with their material interests. But they were noble idealists, well educated, staunch in their beliefs, and they created their own environment in which they maintained a high state of civic commitment. Many of them had taken part in the war against Napoleon on the battlefields of Russia and Europe. They emerged from the experience with not only a selfless love of their country, but with new ideas about its future and its prosperity. This cemented their friendship. While the crowned liberals of their time merely flirted with the ideas of progress, reason, education, and the good of the people, these ideas returned with a vengeance in the shape of the armed rebellion of the Decembrists.

On Tsar Nicholas I's orders the Decembrists and the soldiers who supported them were shot at point-blank range in Senate Square, near the Bronze Horseman, the monument to the first "Europeanizer" of Russia, the founder of the city that became the country's capital and a "window on Europe." There was hidden historical symbolism in this, too.

The empire replied to the revolt of young idealists with grapeshot salvoes; by hanging five of the rebels; by exiling, imprisoning, arresting, or confining dissidents to lunatic asylums for publishing bold statements and "philosophical letters"; for reading and discussing Saint-Simon, Owen, Fourier, and other dangerous "Western heresies"; by creating a gendarmerie and the Third Department of His Imperial Majesty's personal chancellory and finally by creating a system of "thought police."

Count Sergei Uvarov, a former liberal amateur-philosopher who knew the Decembrists and who later became Nicholas's minister of education, tried to bring about a "quiet harmony" between the Imperial Russia of serfdom and education and spiritual life. He proposed an official theory that was to protect this harmony, summed up in the words "Orthodoxy, Autocracy, Nationality (Narodnost)." This ideology explained everything that he deemed it necessary to explain: the inherent and profound piety of the Russian people who carried the image of Christ in them and, therefore, had no need for Western rationalism; the Russian people's special relationship with the tsar, the head of Russia and the Russian Church, in which he was the father concerned daily about his children and responsible for them before God; and, in a similar vein, purely Russian traditional relations between peasants and their masters as between members of the same family, with the landowners assuming fatherly patronage over naive peasants who were incapable of conducting their affairs and living sensibly by themselves. The formula stressed that Western rationalist ideas of social progress, the social contract, democracy, and restructuring of life on new principles were alien to the Russian spirit and the Russian soul and could only lead to senseless and disastrous upheavals. Proof of this, according to the conservatives, was offered by all the revolutions that had taken place in Europe. The formula stressed the danger of idle "speculation," the supremacy of faith over feeble human reason, the need for absolute, "God-given" autocratic power to order Russian life and combat harmful Western influences and intellectual ferment, and the need for all-embracing intellectual and civic supervision. This "direction of thought and spiritual inclinations" was offered as "truly Russian" and patriotic, and the Russian state of Orthodoxy, autocracy, and nationality was to be considered the sacred Fatherland.

The gap between the autocratic state and real life, between the empire and humanity in Russia manifested itself of the constant and fierce opposition between power and spirituality.

The great Russian writers of the nineteenth century — among them, Nikolai Gogol, Ivan Turgenev, Fiodor Dostoyevsky, Shchedrin (Mikhail Saltykov), and Leo Tolstoy — and the course of Russia's development in the nineteenth century reveal the true worth and relevance of this ideology. Even so, its ideas were in one way or another used by conservatives throughout the century, and their echoes can be heard even today. Truly, life and human thought develop in a spiral.

Russian absolutism was without direct analogs in history. The growing centralization of state power, which was a major factor that enabled Russia to overthrow the two-hundred-year Tatar-Mongol yoke in the fifteenth century, and which undermined its productive forces and dramatically delayed its development, had another side to it. "Moscow saved Russia," wrote Alexander Herzen, "by strangling all freedom in Russian life." The supremacy of Moscow made the country's development uneven. Novgorod the Great, a feudal republic, lost its former significance, and other once glorious and wealthy centers of the numerous principalities lost their identity and became drab provincial towns. The dangerous over-concentration of political, social, economic, and cultural life in one place remained after the capital was shifted to St. Petersburg. Although Moscow was officially regarded as the second capital, it could no longer rival its northern neighbor.

St. Petersburg soon became the focus of all government power in the land. In the center of the city — not far from the splendid Winter Palace of the tsars, sumptuous mansions of the courtiers, and magnificent churches — rows of buildings were erected to house ministries and other government departments or to serve as barracks for the regiments of the capital's garrison. Every new autocrat after Peter sought to immortalize himself of herself by adding new features to the capital and actively building up its outskirts. The palaces built as mainly summer residences for the tsars and the parks laid out around them rivaled in their scope and elegance the best of the European parks and architectural ensembles. Peterhof, Gatchina, Tsarskoye Selo, and Pavlovsk — so unlike each other, so strikingly individual — created a precious ring around Petersburg, though each gem in its setting cost the country and its people dearly.

Although Petersburg was close to the northwestern edge of the country — so vast that in the seventeenth century the fastest messenger took a year to travel from one end to the other — the growing bureaucratic machine established full control over the remotest corners of the empire. One of the characters in Maxim Gorky's *My Universities* pinpointed the very essence of the structure of autocratic power. "An invisible thread, a cobweb," the Kazan policeman said confidentially, "issues from the very heart of His Majesty the Emperor, ... passes through His Majesty's ministers, through His Excellency the Governor, and all the ranks down to the likes of me, and even the lowliest of soldiers; this thread connects everything, entangles everything, and the tsar's empire will be sustained by its invisible strength for ages to come." Impartial statistics, however, may be more eloquent than words. While in 1796 the Russian bureaucracy was estimated at 15,000–16,000 (i.e., one official per 2,250 inhabitants), in 1903 that caste numbered 385,000 (one official per 335 inhabitants).

Throughout the centuries during which Petersburg was the capital, the army was growing steadily. In the early twentieth century Russia had an army of 1.5 million men headed by a forty-thousand-strong officer corps, which consisted of noblemen. By that time the army had added the function of policeman to its military duties. While it played a noble mission of liberator, for instance, of the Balkan peoples from the four centuries of Ottoman rule, it was also instrumental in suppressing any signs of struggle for freedom and national independence, not only in the allied empires and their fermenting provinces of Hungary, Poland, and Bohemia, but all over Russia itself. And yet the soldier was a traditionally and universally revered figure. Thus Nicholas II invariably appeared in his army uniform, usually that of a colonel of the Preobrazhensky Regiment, the first of the Russian Guards. A Petersburg directory for 1899 had information on the War Ministry and the army immediately after the emperor's family, and before the data on the emperor's court, the State Council, the Ministerial Committee, individual ministries, and government institutions.

An equally important role in the life of the empire was played by the department of police and the Ministry of the Interior, "states within a state," which had a 100,000-strong corps of gendarmes and policemen. Far from outliving itself, the tradition that had its roots in the notorious reign of Ivan the Terrible, who had created a far-flung apparatus of violence, repression, and spying, reached its apogee by the beginning of the twentieth century. Police spying on political suspects was widely practiced. A far-flung network of gendarme and security departments existed in all the provinces. This huge state bureaucracy and the military and police machine zealously guarded the regime and its political superstructure. The Church, which had become an arm of officialdom, had a legion of 200,000 priests. Peter had eliminated the office of patriarch and proclaimed himself head of the Russian Orthodox Church, thereby acquiring supreme spiritual power over his subjects. The Church was ruled by the Holy Synod, a council of hierarchs appointed and replaced by the tsar on the recommendation of the Supreme Procurator, his personal representative, something like a Minister of the Orthodox Faith who ran Church affairs in much the same way as any bureaucrat would; his metropolitans and archbishops could advise but could not take part in decision making.

Surveying Russian history, one gets the impression that the country was in a state of internal war that continued for centuries and that did more harm than had invasions from abroad. Comparing the consequences of the Tatar-Mongol invasion with those of the reign of Ivan the Terrible, the historian Nikolai Karamzin wrote: "If Batu Khan's yoke humiliated the spirit of the Russians, the reign of Ivan hardly lifted their spirit." He dwelt only on irreparable damage to the morale of the Russian people, but the physical and material losses were incalculable, too. Let it be remembered that in the centuries of the Golden Horde and its successors, including the last, the Crimean Khannate, millions of Russians and Ukranians were driven into slavery and sold like cattle in Oriental bazaars. Hardly had it recovered from the swords and arrows of the Tatars than the country was again the scene of a bloodbath staged by the frenzied tsar who murdered his own son, aided by his brainchild, the corps of *oprichnina*, whose traditions lasted practically into the nineteenth century. With huge manpower resources at their disposal, the Russian monarchs who succeeded Ivan the Terrible treated humans like pawns whom they readily sacrificed. This was so not only in times of war, but also in peacetime, when abject poverty, epidemics, famine, and conscripted labor claimed thousands upon thousands of lives every year. The empire grew and expanded on their bones.

The traditionally low living standards of the working people and the mass of peasantry were aggravated by political disfranchisement and were closely linked with the preservation of the Russian monarchy, the main survival of feudalism and serfdom in the country's social and political life. The policy pursued by the autocratic state embittered the minds and hearts, which according to Vlas Doroshevich, the famous liberal journalist at the turn of the century, "put bombs in hands that would be much happier wielding a pen." Violence begat violence.

The capital of empire, linked with other powers not only by diplomatic relations, but also by the kinship bonds of the Romanov dynasty with many other royal families of Europe — German, British, Danish, Greek — the capital where the sounds of bands on parade, solemn speeches and ceremonies, the roar of fireworks to greet an endless stream of visiting dignitaries never stopped — in this capital a different kind of music was heard more and more loudly with every passing year: the explosions of handmade bombs, rifle shots, and the swishing of the Cossacks' whips.

The racecourse in Krasnoye Selo. Nicholas II is among the spectators on the balcony. 1906
The summer camp of the guards was situated in Krasnoye Selo, and the arrival of the tsar, recalled General Ignatyev, "turned the camp into a society feast for several days. In Krasnoye Selo, one could still watch the horse races as described by Leo Tolstoy in *Anna Karenina*. The tsar handed prizes to the best marksmen, riders, and even cooks in front of the grandstand. After the race everyone jumped into carriages drawn by one, two, or three horses and rushed to the Krasnoselsky Theatre where the prima ballerina Kshesinskaya shone, admired by all three of her successive royal lovers — Nicholas II, his young uncle Sergei Mikhailovich, and the youthful Andrei, the younger brother of Kirill, the future pretender to the throne."

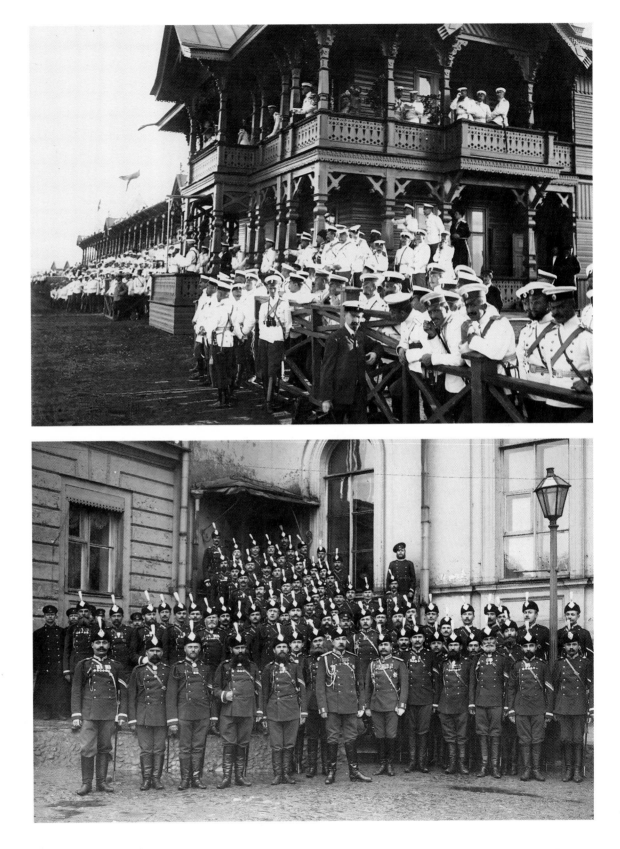

A group of gendarmes at the Baltic Station. 1900s

In the first two decades of the twentieth century, which saw the humiliation of the Russo-Japanese War, Bloody Sunday of January 22 (9 o.s.), 1905, the massive revolutionary upheavals of 1905–07, and subsequent executions, the World War, court intrigues, and the strange power of Rasputin, the tsar's autocracy discredited itself in the eyes of its compatriots and in the eyes of the world, and its disastrous role in the country's history became ever clearer. There was no real chance of the Russian monarchy surviving. The dramatic events of February 1917 followed inevitably.

Tsar Nicholas II with the tsarina, Alexandra Feodorovna (Alix of Hesse-Darmstadt). Late 1890s

Completing a national census form in January 1897, Nicholas gave his rank as "the first nobleman of Russia," his occupation as "the master of the Russian land," and his side activity as "landowner." Alexandra Feodorovna described her occupation and side activity as "mistress of the Russian land" and "governess of workhouses."

The Romanov dynasty traced its lineage to Mikhail, son of Metropolitan Filaret, a representative of an old Boyar family. He was elected Russian tsar at the Zemstvo Assembly held in Moscow in 1613 after the death of Tsar Boris Godunov, which was followed by the "time of troubles."

Following are the reigns of the Romanov tsars: Mikhail, 1613—45; Alexei, 1645—76; Fiodor III, 1676–82; Ivan V and Peter I, ruled jointly 1682–96 (under regent Sophia, 1682—89); Peter I (ruled alone), 1696—1725; Catherine I, 1725—27; Peter II, 1727–30; Anna Ioannovna, 1730–40; Ivan VI, 1740–41; Elizabeth, 1741–61; Peter III, 1761–62; Catherine II, 1762–96; Paul I, 1796–1801; Alexander I, 1801–25; Nicholas I, 1825–55; Alexander II, 1855–81; Alexander III, 1881–94; Nicholas II, 1894–1917.

Tsar Nicholas II with son, Alexei. 1913

The joy at the birth of a long-awaited heir (the fifth child) was marred by the discovery of the tsarevich's grave ailment: hemophilia. The incurable disease and the parents' constant fear for the life of their child was not only a family tragedy but a major reason for the rise of Grigory Rasputin whose presence was thought by the empress to be favorable for her son's health.

The tsar's family. Left to right: Grand Duchesses Tatyana, Maria, Anastasia, and Olga. Center (sitting): Tsarina Alexandra Feodorovna, Tsar Nicholas II, and Tsarevich Alexei. 1913

Every son of a tsar drew an annual allowance of 150,000 rubles, a birthday present of 1 million rubles on his coming of age, and 235,000 after marriage. His wife got 40,000 rubles a year, and children between 50,000 and 150,000 rubles (until they came of age). By comparison, a factory worker's annual wage was, on average, 246 rubles a year (in 1910); the average incomes of peasants were even lower.

ABOVE:

The Imperial Family at the consecration of a dock dedicated to Tsarevich Alexei. Kronstadt. July 14 (1 o.s.), 1914

Nicholas II and members of the Imperial Family leaving to embark on a boat on Petrovskaya Embankment. August 1912

During their trips around the country and walks in the parks of Peterhof and Tsarskoye Selo, the emperor and his family were guarded by the official escort, as well as by plainclothes agents of the palace police, part of the Palace Commandant's Administration. They numbered more than two hundred fifty.

123

ABOVE:

Members of the Imperial Family playing tennis. Left, Nicholas II. 1912

Nicholas II with children on the beach of the Gulf of Finland. Early 1900s

OVERLEAF:

Military parade on May Day in the Field of Mars. 1903

From the first year of his reign, Nicholas II revived the May Day parades marking the end of the winter military season, a tradition that had been abandoned under Alexander II. Open stands for the public were built over the whole length of the Field of Mars. Only well-off people could afford to be there. The stands were much favored by society ladies wishing to display their Paris spring fashions. General Alexei Ignatyev left an eye-witness account of the ceremony:

"After inspecting the troops, the tsar stopped before the imperial grandstand accompanied only by a bugler from his escort who stood a little behind and to one side. He wore a scarlet Cossack's coat and sat on a gray horse.

"Two red lines of Cossacks opened the march of the troops. Following the escort, the Battalion of the Pavlovskoye Military School goose-stepped by, then a combined battalion headed by the company of the Corps of Pages, whose helmets brought back memories of bygone times.

"In the interval that followed, the band of the Preobrazhensky Regiment moved into the middle of the field, and then the Guard marched in a formation called 'Alexander columns,' which dated back to Napoleonic times.

"In the artillery units that followed the infantry, one was struck by the neatly harnessed, strong and well-fed horses selected by color in truly Russian taste: first chestnut, then bay, and then black.

"After a minute's break a mass of mounted troops glittering in the sun appeared at the edge of the field from the direction of the Mikhailovsky Castle. This was our First Cuirassier Division of the Guards advancing at an ambling pace."

Members of the State Council and the First Duma arriving at the Winter Palace to be received by the emperor. Palace Square.
May 10 (April 27 o.s.), 1906

The Winter Palace contained 1,050 rooms with a total floor area of 46,000 square meters. It had 1,945 windows, 1,786 doors, 117 staircases, and 329 chimneys. For 150 years it served as the winter residence of almost all the tsars. Nicholas II lived here from September or October through May every year for the first ten years of his reign. Between 1904 and 1917, when the emperor chose the Alexander Palace in Tsarskoye Selo as his chief residence, the Winter Palace came to life only during the tsar's occasional visits and gala receptions.

RIGHT:
Main office of the Ministry of the Imperial Court and Crown Properties.
39 Liteiny Prospekt. 1900s

The Ministry of the Imperial Court managed the huge imperial household and raised funds for the tsar and his relatives. At the beginning of the twentieth century the upkeep of the ministry, which had a staff of 1,300, cost the government treasury from 12.7 to 17 million rubles annually.

OPPOSITE:
Footmen in the Winter Palace garden. 1900s

By 1914 the imperial court employed 5 chief stewards, 6 chief chasseurs, 103 stewards, 45 equerries, 20 chasseurs, up to 400 chamberlains, 40 gentlemen of the bedchamber — all of these being persons of a very high rank and station — and other court officers. The wives and daughters of these people were often court ladies: a score of ladies-in-waiting, several maids of honor, more than 250 maids. There were, of course, numerous footmen, etc., as well.

Grigory Rasputin with Major General Prince Putiatin and Colonel Loman, Commandant of the Tsarskoye Selo Palace. 1912

Son of a peasant from the Tobolsk Gubernia in Siberia who acquired the reputation of a holy man and a *starets* (unordained man of religion), Rasputin was introduced to Nicholas II in November 1905 and for the next decade became closely associated with the Imperial Family. Possessed of powers to influence people — especially women — a powerful physique, and undoubted gift of suggestion, Rasputin developed an extraordinary influence on Empress Alexandra. The small summer house of Anna Alexandrovna Vyrubova, a maid of honor at the empress's court, situated in Tsarskoye Selo, became a place of gatherings of mystically inclined admirers of Rasputin. Rumors of his licentious ways and debauchery spread around Petersburg, causing widespread discontent in various circles. Prime Minister Stolypin waged a losing battle against him by presenting the empress with reports of Rasputin's misdeeds: the notes went into the fire. Kokovtsev, Stolypin's successor, exerted immense efforts to discredit the *starets*. He succeeded, after a debate at the Duma, in having Rasputin exiled to his home village in Siberia in 1912. But Rasputin was soon summoned to Petersburg by the Imperial Family. In 1916 the legendary man was murdered by a group of monarchist conspirators headed by Vladimir Purishkevich. It happened at the palace of Prince Felix Yusupov. The actual cause of death was neither cyanide nor the bullet wounds, but drowning: the conspirators threw his body through a hole in the ice on the river. His involvement in the episode earned Prince Yusupov great notoriety. The actor Alexander Vertinsky recalled that, when Yusupov was living in Paris as an émigré, people flocked to his salon to look at the man who had killed Rasputin.

ABOVE:

Anna Alexandrovna Vyrubova, maid of honor to Empress Alexandra Feodorovna. 1900s

Khamsaran Badmayev (Piotr Alexandrovich after his conversion to Orthodoxy), member of Rasputin's circle. 1912–13

PRECEDING PAGES:

Nicholas II delivers a speech from the throne on the opening of the Duma. Winter Palace. May 10 (April 27 o.s.), 1906

According to the Principal Laws of the Russian Empire, adopted by the Duma in 1906–07, this body was a representative legislature with limited power. The second, but superior, legislative body was the State Council, which could reject or amend the recommendations of the Duma. The highest authority was the emperor, who ratified the decisions of the Duma and the State Council and had the right to dissolve either body.

Meeting of the State Council in the Nobles' Assembly Building. 1906

All the members of the State Council, the supreme legislative and consultative body in Russia, were appointed by the tsar from among the court, army, and bureaucratic élite (after 1906 half of the members were appointed). Pavel Miliukov, the leader of the Constitutional Democrats, wrote: "It was enough to look at the realm of somnolent, mumbling ghosts to feel as if in a musty, moss-grown vault that had survived by a fluke in the midst of new and alien forms of life."

Elections to City Council. Polling station on Liteiny Prospekt.
November 29 (November 16 o.s.), 1909

ABOVE:

**A group of the members of the Fourth Duma from the Petersburg
Gubernia: A. E. Badayev, N. G. Yevseyev, L. A. Zinovyev,
A. S. Postnikov, 1912–14**

The house of the Governing Senate,
the supreme judiciary and supervisory body. 1911

The State Bank. Ekaterininsky
Canal. 1900s

The Ministry of Finance. 43–47
Moika Embankment. Early 1900s

State Supervision Building.
76 Moika Embankment. 1911

The Ministry of Education.
2–5 Chernyshova Square. 1900s

District Court Building.
4 Liteiny Prospekt. 1910–11

OPPOSITE:

Sergei Yulyevich Witte, minister of finance and chairman of the Council of Ministers between October 1905 and April 1906. 1905

"When considering the activity of Witte," wrote Anatoly Koni, "one cannot help seeing that it is informed with the idea that the best form of government is unlimited autocracy relying on able, energetic, and knowledgeable ministers with years of experience in their particular fields and who can choose suitable assistants."

Piotr Arkadyevich Stolypin, minister of the interior, chairman of the Council of Ministers. 1906

Stolypin's career peaked at a difficult time for Russia. He was a devoted monarchist, chairman of the Council of Ministers, and interior minister from 1906 to 1911, and he exercised his powers with determination. He is chiefly remembered for his attempted agrarian reform, the pogroms staged by the Black Hundreds, and the grim period of reaction after the Revolution of 1905 was crushed. But it was his strong will and determination and his negative attitude toward Rasputin that had turned Nicholas and Alexandra and the imperial couple's milieu against him. On September 14 (1 o.s.), 1911, he was mortally wounded in Kiev by Dmitry Bogrov, who had strange links with the security police. During a somewhat curtailed and confused interrogation, he declared himself an anarchist, but it became known after February 1917 that, prior to the assassination, he had been filed in the police archives as a member of the SR party and a double secret agent.

Members of the Foreign Affairs Ministry: Prince Grigory Nikolayevich Trubetskoi and Baron Mavry Fabianovich Shilling. 1897–1900

The staff of the Foreign Affairs Ministry before the Revolution of 1917 included thirty-nine barons, thirty-two princes, a dozen counts, and even a grand duke.

Sergei Dmitriyevich Sazonov, minister of foreign affairs. 1912

"A Russian among Russians when it came to defending the interests of his country," wrote George Buchanan, former British ambassador to Russia, "he was a loyal friend of Great Britain until his last day as Minister of Foreign Affairs, until July 1916 when the Emperor, unfortunately for himself and for Russia, was advised to replace him by Sturmer."

Alexander Grigoryevich Bulygin, minister of the interior. 1905

OPPOSITE, ABOVE:

Admiral Ivan Konstantinovich Grigorovich, the marine minister (center), with high-ranking officials of the Marine Ministry. 1914

OPPOSITE, BELOW:

Vladimir Alexandrovich Sukhomlinov, the war minister, with his wife, officers, and instructors. 1910

In June 1915, five years after this photograph was taken, Sukhomlinov was replaced as war minister by Alexei Polivanov. The following year he was arrested and charged with mishandling the Russian Army's preparation for the war. Sentenced to life imprisonment in 1917, he was released in 1918 on account of his advanced age. He emigrated shortly afterward.

A group of officers at the walls of the Peter and Paul Fortress. 1911

"The chronicle of this huge mass of stone rising from the Neva opposite the Winter Palace speaks of nothing but murders and torture, of prisoners buried alive, condemned to slow death or driven to insanity in dank, gloomy, solitary cells," wrote an inmate of the Russian Bastille, one of the leaders of world anarchism, Prince Piotr Kropotkin, who came from the Rurikovich family. Over two centuries thousands of people deemed to be dangerous by the autocrats passed through the dungeons of the Peter and Paul Fortress. Among them were Tsarevich Alexei, the son of Peter I, statesmen and generals Biron, Osterman, Münnich, A. N. Radishchev (the first Russian revolutionary and writer), the Decembrists K. F. Ryleyev, P. I. Pestel, M. P. Bestuzhev-Riumin, S. P. Trubetskoi, and others, the members of the Petrashevsky Circle, including the great nineteenth-century writer Fiodor Dostoyevsky, N. G. Chernyshevsky, D. I. Pisarev, the Narodniki (Populists) and revolutionary democrats M. A. Bakunin, P. N. Tkachov, A. I. Zheliabov, V. N. Figner, S. A. Perovskaya, Alexander Ulyanov (the brother of Lenin), and revolutionaries of the third generation including N. E. Bauman, V. P. Nogin, I. I. Radchenko, P. N. Lepeshinsky, and others. Among the prisoners of the Peter and Paul Fortress were A. M. Gorky, N. I. Kareyev, N. F. Annensky. After the February Revolution it was the prison for former tsarist ministers, and from October 1917 for the ministers of the Provisional Government.

ABOVE:

Peasants who brought their wares to Sennoi Market have their papers checked. 1900s

CENTER:

Headquarters of the Detached Gendarmes Corps. 40 Furstatskaya Street. 1914

From the buildings in Furstatskaya Street and the Fontanka Embankment in Petersburg, where the Gendarmes Corps and the Police Department were housed, invisible threads spread throughout Russia, entangling it in an intricate cobweb of spying and surveillance. The Police Department and the Gendarmes Corps spread their tentacles beyond Russia's borders. Russian political detectives were active in several countries in Europe and Asia, and went as far afield as America. In 1905–17 secret services kept watch over four or five thousand political émigrés from Russia who lived in Western Europe alone.

ABOVE:
**Austrian Emperor Franz
Josef I arrives at
Petersburg's Nikolayevsky
Station.
April 1897**

CENTER:
**Italian King Victor
Emmanuel III visits
Petersburg. July 1902**

RIGHT:
**Spanish Infante Don
Fernando in Petersburg.
August 1908**

A sculpture symbolizing the friendship between France and Russia. Mikhailovskaya Street. 1902

The capital donned its festive garb for the visits of foreign dignitaries. Bedecked with flags, busts, archways, garlands, sculptural groups, masts, and carpets, and illuminated with gas lights, it presented a cheery look.

ABOVE:

Frederick VIII, king of Denmark, visiting Peterhof. 1909

OVERLEAF:

The arrival of the German Emperor Wilhelm II and his retinue at the manoeuvers in Krasnoye Selo. In the carriage are the emperor's consort, Augusta Victoria and the Russian Empress Alexandra Feodorovna. 1906

The first squadron of the British Royal Navy in Petersburg. June 1914

Admiral David Beatty (second from right), Commander of the Royal British Squadron, with his staff. Kronstadt. June 23 (10 o.s.), 1914

George Buchanan, British ambassador to Russia (second from left) and embassy staff. 1914

ABOVE:

The American Squadron in Petersburg. The battleship *Kansas*. Kronstadt. 1911

RIGHT:

The United States Embassy. 34 Furstatskaya Street. 1913

OPPOSITE:

American and Russian seamen exchange handshakes. 1911

It Could Be Any Day

The University Embankment. 1900s

OVERLEAF:
Canteen for the poor. Harbor on Vasilyevsky Island. 1911

Inside the Passage. 48 Nevsky Prospekt. 1900

Lounge of the Egorov Public Baths.
11 Kazachy Lane. 1900s

IT COULD BE ANY DAY

Mstislav Dobuzhinsky, a brilliant painter and writer of memoirs, recalled the many diverse sounds constantly heard in Petersburg's streets in the late nineteenth century: "Church bells tolled on holidays, military bands with trumpets and drums would often pass, and in courtyards vendors hawked their wares — and all these sounds were melodious. The only hideous sound was made by the rails being dragged by work horses on the cobblestone pavement." This mighty symphony expressed the character of the city, the diverse and motley life of the metropolis.

The people of Petersburg woke up in the morning to the wailing of factory sirens, which was repeated three times, hurrying workmen to factories. They streamed in their thousands to the factories and mills that formed a tight ring around the city. In the four decades since the abolition of serfdom, the number of factories more than doubled: from 374 to 878. In addition to the old giants — the Putilovsky, Izhorsky, the Nevsky shipyard, and other industries — there sprang up the Obukhovsky Steel Works, Phoenix, the Nevskaya Thread Factory, and the Malo-Okhtinskaya Mill, Treugolnik and Skorokhod, which produced rubber and leather shoes, tobacco and chemical enterprises, and large print shops. On the eve of the Revolution of 1905, the capital's work force numbered 250,000–260,000, one-tenth of the industrial proletariat of Russia. A city of court noblemen, the military and the bureaucrats, Petersburg was turning into a city of workingmen.

The first to appear in the streets every day were the industrious Petersburg janitors, who got up early in the morning to bring water and firewood for the citizens, to clear the sidewalks of snow and sprinkle them with sand, to remove horse dung and mud and, in the summer, to wash the pavement. All these chores kept them busy throughout the day. At night, when the gates and doors were closed, janitors had to help home residents whose socializing and partying had lasted a little too long.

At dawn, the main transport artery of Petersburg came to life. The swift and full-flowing Neva River was, in the early twentieth century, still handling the bulk of the cargo arriving in the capital, most of which was firewood and timber. A modern city dweller who has the benefit of central heating can hardly imagine the huge amount of firewood devoured daily by the ovens, chimneys, and boiler rooms of Petersburg. The Neva and its numerous branches and canals were clogged with heavy barges piled high with neatly stacked logs. Instead of being sent back, the huge wooden barges were often taken apart, dried, and sawed into firewood.

The capital's turnover of cargo increased dramatically with the opening of the Morskoi Canal and the construction, in 1885, of St. Petersburg port, which in 1900–13 handled more than two thousand ships from overseas and about thirty-five hundred freight-and-passenger and coastal steamers every season (the river was navigable about two hundred twenty days a year). Construction materials came in an uninterrupted stream: marble, granite, cobblestone, gravel, and especially limestone, which was used to pave the sidewalks. Petersburg's old-timers remember their light surface with, here and there, imprints of prehistoric creatures. Limestone was also used in foundations and plinths and as a concrete filler, facing stone, etc. Houses mushroomed in Petersburg. As of 1910, the city's housing stock amounted to 37,523 buildings, of which 15,121 were of stone — the remaining houses were made of wood. In 1910–14 the capital lived through

A ship being loaded in the Petersburg commercial port. 1914
Before the Morskoi (Maritime) Canal was built, ships from all parts of the world were unloaded on Kotlin Island at the Kronstadt port, from where cargoes were delivered by shallow-draft vessels to Petersburg. The 27-kilometer journey from Kronstadt to the capital often took as long as the journey from England or America, which hindered foreign trade. After the opening of the canal in the late nineteenth century, the Petersburg port burgeoned and by 1912 the length of all its piers amounted to 62 kilometers, and the annual cargo turnover varied from 4 to 5.6 million tons, depending on the year's wheat harvest.

Cutting ice on the Neva at the Nikolayevsky Bridge. 1900s
"Here and there (and almost everywhere) on the vast expanse of the river covered by Arctic ice almost one meter thick, square and rectangular holes were cut. They were roped off. All day long men used iron bars with axe-shaped ends to cut huge blocks of ice, a meter and a half long and 70 centimeters thick. They were aquamarine, green, amazingly gentle of tint, translucent ice prisms. More and more prisms were taken out of the water, loaded on sleds which came in an endless stream." (From *The Notes of a Petersburg Old-Timer* by Lev Uspensky).

a building boom. Every year, in the spring, more than 100,000 seasonal workers came to Petersburg. The focus of building activity was on the Petersburg Side of town.

But the most notable presence in the city were the merchants. As soon as you found yourself in the central thoroughfares — the Nevsky and Voznesensky Prospekts, Morskaya, Sadovaya, and Gorokhovaya streets — you couldn't help recalling the words of Makar Devushkin, a character from Dostoyevsky, expressing his wonderment at the scene: "What wealthy shops and stores: everything glitters and shines, materials, flowers in glass cases, hats with ribbons. One might think that all this is laid out just for display, but no: there are people who buy all these things and give them to their wives." Painted shop windows, notices, advertisements, which often covered the façades of buildings from top to bottom, beckoned, tempted, and lured you. In addition to a multitude of little shops and all sorts of stalls, which crowded and jostled each other, major shops sprang up to form a metropolitan trade center: Gostiny Dvor, which, as the *Rossiysky Magazine* reported in 1792, had no equals in Europe; Apraksin Dvor with one of the biggest emporia in Europe; the Passage, which accommodated rows of stalls, as well as exhibition and theater halls, seamstresses' and other workshops. In the most crowded and bustling places the ubiquitous hawkers scurried with trays, boxes, and carts, offering wares that ranged from pastries to balloons. Bazaars and flea markets, always noisy and crowded, usually sprang up next to churches.

To ensure an uninterrupted flow of goods, and to supply hospitals and pharmacies, numerous snack bars, pubs, and restaurants, huge quantities of ice from the Neva were needed. During winter huge containers in the marine port, freight railway stations, stores and shops, cafés, hotels, and private houses were stocked with ice cubes. This made it possible to preserve perishable goods in the warmest weather, to offer refreshing soft drinks or champagne on ice, and to manufacture delicious ice cream, which was very much in demand.

The bustling activity was not confined only to the squares and streets filled with shoppers; the doors of the many banks and banking offices, too, opened promptly on time. They occupied twenty-eight out of the fifty houses on Nevsky Prospekt, on the short stretch from the Admiralty to Anichkov Bridge. Situated in this financial center were the governing boards of Russia's major banks. The life of these institutions, like that of many other private and government offices, agencies, departments, and ministries, died down in the evening. Files were put away until the following morning, safes and drawers were locked, and lights were put out. The offi-

cials and the clerks hurried home. But in other places work was only beginning. Last-minute articles were being finished in newspaper offices and information was processed, typesetters and proofreaders hurried to their workplaces in order to provide the citizens with the latest news gathered during the day by ubiquitous reporters.

The city fell asleep as the printers clicked, the horse-drawn and electric-driven trams rang, and hoofs clattered on the cobblestones as cabs took people home from theaters and parties.

The city transformed itself with every new season. At Christmastime, bazaars selling fir trees sprang up much to the delight of children. At the tail end of winter troikas carried their jolly passengers who were "seeing winter out." The snow grew thin, its sludgy remains were hurriedly taken away, sleds and high felt boots were put away until next winter. The city, filled with the chirping of birds and the clatter of wheel carts, was preparing for the main spring holiday, Easter, with the solemn ringing of church bells, processions with icons, painted eggs, and everybody embracing and greeting each other with the words: "Christ is risen!" — "Risen indeed!"

A few weeks sped by, and following the breaking of ice on Lake Ladoga in May, the long-awaited summer came. By Whitsunday, not only the quiet city parks and gardens, but the woodlands in the outskirts put on their lush foliage. As summer came into its own, the bright greenery, like all spring colors, gradually faded. The janitors had to sprinkle the pavements more and more often, and gusts of wind drove trampled and dried horse dung through the streets.

Petersburg was deserted in summer, the time of vacations. The rich went to their country estates or to spas abroad, and others went to dachas. The dacha communities were filled with children's voices, laughter, the scolding of nannies and governesses, and the sophisticated aura of smartly dressed city dwellers. During the period "the city was taken over by cooks, janitors, and house-maids," wrote Dobuzhinsky. "They sat on benches near the gates, shelling sunflower seeds. The merry house painters, who flooded Petersburg in summer, belted out songs to the sound of an accordion. This was 'Peter', the city of working men."

Airman Piotr Nikolayevich Nesterov meets the staff of the newspaper *Vecherneye Vremia*. 1913
The outstanding Russian air-force pilot, one of the founders of aerobatics, Captain Nesterov was the first to bank a plane while turning and to perform a "loop" (the "Nesterov loop") on September 10 (August 27 o.s.), 1913. He was killed in an air battle on September 9 (August 26 o.s.), 1914, when he struck the enemy with the hull of his aircraft and so downed an Austrian plane.

Welding workers at the Ludwig Nobel Engineering and Iron works. 13–15 Sampsoniyevskaya Embankment. 1910

ABOVE:
A shop at the radio and telephone factory under the Maritime Department. 1912

CENTER:
Posters being prepared at the Marx printing shop. 29 Izmailovsky Prospekt. 1897

RIGHT:
Workers of the George Borman chocolate-candy factory preparing sugar syrup. 16 English Prospekt. 1900s

OPPOSITE:
A workshop manufacturing cartridge shells. 1900s

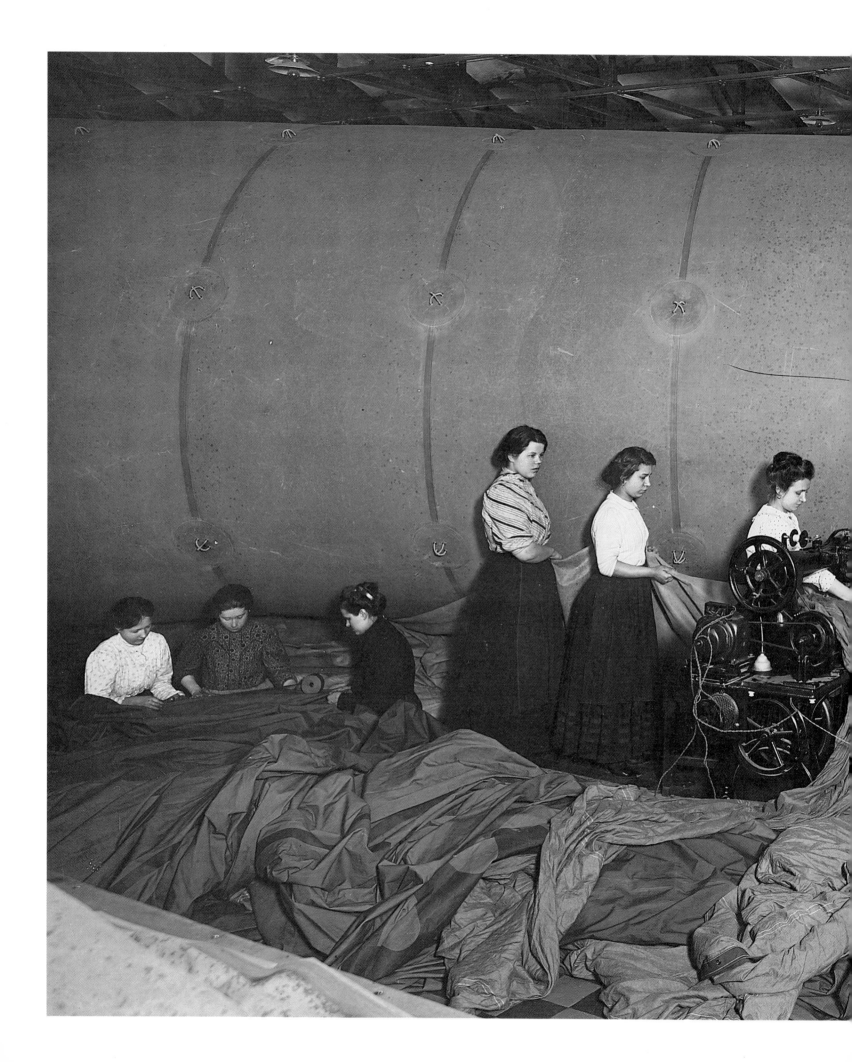

Women workers at the Russian-American rubber factory making a cover for an air balloon. 1911

Sorting shop for old rags, part of the Expedition for the Manufacture of Government Papers. 144 Fontanka Embankment. 1900s

Founded in 1818, the Expedition for the Manufacture of Government Papers was the only enterprise in the capital that both produced paper and used it in printing, mainly for the government. In the early twentieth century the Expedition, equipped with the most up-to-date Russian-made and imported machinery, set world standards in printing. Skilled personnel were trained by the Expedition's nineyear school, most of whose pupils were children of Expedition employees. After six years of general education, the trainees took one of the specialized courses in paper making, photography, and printing.

Laying of wooden paving blocks on the Palace Embankment. Early 1900s.

From the times of Peter I, paving the streets was the duty of the owners of the adjacent lots. They were not allowed to begin roadwork before May 15 or to block the whole width of the street for repairs. Among the various types of pavements — cobblestone, macadam, etc. — wooden blocks were particularly notable. The first time they were ever used in the world was in 1832 to pave Nevsky Prospekt, the Bolshaya and Malaya Morskaya streets, the English, Palace, and French embankments, the Millionnay Street, Kamenno-Ostrovsky Prospekt, and others, Liteiny, Zagorodny, and Vladimirsky Prospekts, the embankments of the Moika, Fontanka, the Ekaterininsky Canal, and other wealthier quarters were partly paved with wooden blocks. Their advantage was that they muffled the clatter of horses' hoofs and cart wheels. But they could cause a lot of trouble during floods, when the water dislodged them.

Reconstruction of Anichkov Bridge across the Fontanka.
1906–08

The operations hall of the United Bank (St. Petersburg branch) 23 Nevsky Prospekt. 1912

Mortgaging of real estate at the Mortgaging Society (Liteiny branch). 78 Nevsky Prospekt. May 1903

Petersburg Mutual Credit Society. The private-safe vaults. September 1913

The Private Commercial Bank in St. Petersburg. 1 Nevsky Prospekt. 1910

Siberian Trade Bank (St. Petersburg branch). 20 Nevsky Prospekt. 1907–14

The Stock Exchange. Late 1890s

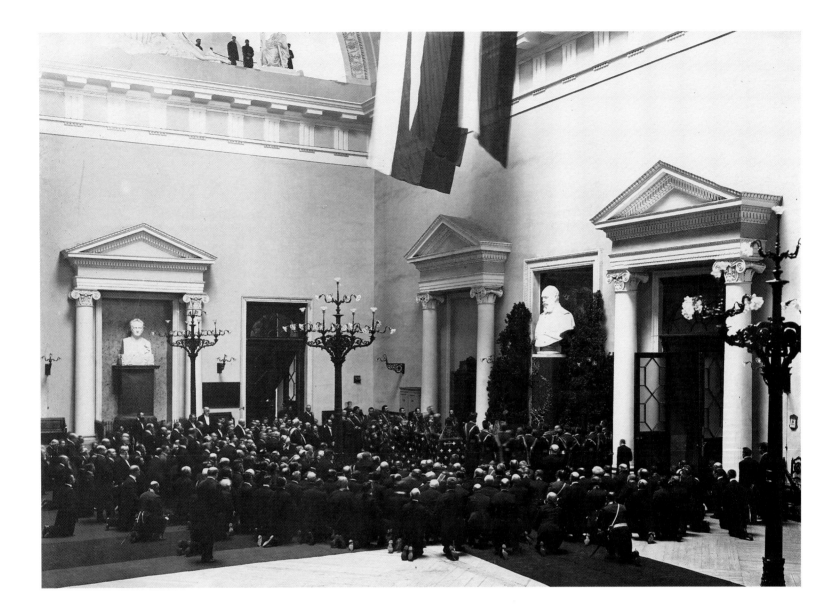

**Church service in the main hall of the Stock Exchange to mark
the unveiling of a bust of Emperor Alexander III. 1903**

ABOVE:

The show window of a wicker-basket shop. 1900s

OPPOSITE, ABOVE:

Window of the hardware shop of F. Zolotov. 25 Nevsky Prospekt. 1900s

RIGHT:

Stalls at Apraksin Dvor. Before 1914

Apraksin Dvor was the second largest of the twenty marketplaces in Petersburg in 1913. It contained more than five hundred emporia, which sold furs, ready-made clothes, hats, china, furniture, shoes, rugs, leather, hardware, etc. The biggest marketplace was the Alexandrovsky Market in Voznesensky Prospekt, which had about eight hundred emporia, plus its famous flea markets.

OPPOSITE, BELOW:

"Live" advertising of the Singer Sewing-Machine Company shop. 10 Zagorodny Prospekt. 1904

Textile shop. 1910s

**Secondhand shop of the Evangelical Society for the Religious and
Moral Instruction of Protestants in St. Petersburg.
7 Narvskaya Square. 1910s**

The vegetable warehouse and shop. 1905

RIGHT:

Vendors at the equestrian monument to Peter I. 1900s

BELOW, LEFT:

Advertisement of the "Monopole" trading company. 1900s

BELOW, RIGHT:

A woman selling herrings. 1900s

OPPOSITE, ABOVE:

Vendors in the Field of Mars. 1895

Foodshops played the leading role in Petersburg's retail trade both in terms of their number and turnover. They accounted for 10,418 out of the 15,430 shops (as of 1900). The largest volume of trade was in farm produce, especially bread. In addition to wholesale companies, the capital had about 1,000 bakeries and confectioneries. Meat, fish, and dairy products were sold in 2,305 shops.

"Innumerable hawkers and street artisans throng the streets," wrote Mstislav Dobuzhinsky. "Vendors with samovars on trays who sold tea, knife sharpeners, glaziers, sellers of balloons, Tatars who sold gowns, floor-polishers — you name it, and their white aprons, peaked caps, homespun coats, felt boots (which sometimes had red decorations) and the various paraphernalia and tools of their trades — all this enlivened the scene."

OPPOSITE, BELOW:

Shoemakers at a flea market near the Obvodny Canal. Early 1900s

**Rummage sale.
December 1903**

ABOVE:
Dominique restaurant. 24 Nevsky Prospekt. 1900s

OPPOSITE, ABOVE:
Building workers at lunch break. 1900s

OPPOSITE, BELOW:
Distribution of free meals. 1900s

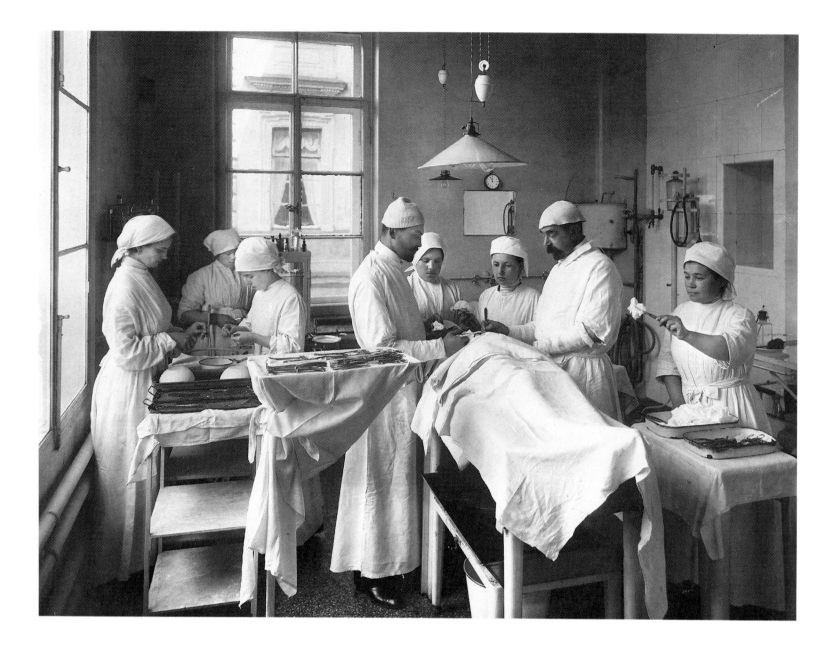

ABOVE:

In an operating theater at the Prince Peter von Oldenburg Children's Hospital. 8 Ligovskaya Street. 1912

OPPOSITE, ABOVE:

Pediatric patients at the Prince Peter von Oldenburg Children's Hospital. 8 Ligovskaya Street. 1900s

OPPOSITE, BELOW:

Obukhovskaya Hospital. 106 Fontanka Embankment. 1913

Founded in 1779, the Obukhovskaya Hospital was the first hospital for civilians. By the beginning of the century, it had three hundred hospital beds. Among the famous medical specialists who worked there were N. I. Pirogov, A. A. Nechayev, I. I. Grekov.

By 1900 Petersburg had twelve hospitals (five general ones, one for children, one for infectious diseases, three psychiatric and two veneral-disease hospitals). Between them they had 10,600 beds. In 1911 construction began of the largest general hospital, named after Peter the Great (now the Mechnikovskaya Hospital). In addition, there were eleven outpatient hospitals, which offered medical services free of charge and were manned by forty municipal doctors.

ABOVE:

People queueing up for a workers' hostel. 1900s

Bedroom in the hostel for workers. Glukhoozerskaya Street. 1900s
This workers' hostel, set up by the St. Petersburg temperance authority on the
premises of a former glassworks, had a bedroom for two hundred people.
A customer had to show his passport and pay 5 kopecks.

**A Jewish community center and synagogue. 2 Lermontovsky
Prospekt. 1910s**

Mosque. 7 Kronversky Prospekt. 1910–12

**Worshipers in a Buddhist pagoda. Staraya Derevnia.
91 Lipovaya Lane. 1900–10.**

ABOVE:

A fireman in a special suit preparing to enter a smoke-filled building. 1900s

RIGHT:

Porters at the Nikolayevsky Railway Station. 1910–12

OPPOSITE, ABOVE:

Firemen lifting a motorcar that had fallen into the Moika River near the house at No 40. Early 1900s

OPPOSITE, BELOW:

The mansion of Baron V. B. Fredericks. 23 Konnogvardeisky Lane. 1908

OPPOSITE, CLOCKWISE FROM TOP LEFT:
Merchant at the Gardner Porcelain and Glass Trading Company. 1911
Housemaid. 1910–12
Chimney sweep. 1910–13
Foreman. Early 1900s
Cook. 1900s

A man with a camera. Early 1910s

OVERLEAF:
City cabbies. 1899
Mstislav Dobuzhinsky remembers: "Petersburg's cabbies, popularly known as *vankas* were part of every street scene. From time immemorial they wore a blue peasant coat reaching to their heels and an oilcloth hat, a flat, low cylinder widening at the bottom with upturned brims (with an obligatory copper buckle in front). In winter they wore fur hats with a coarse-cloth, sometimes velvet square top. And they had such wonderful multicolored decorative belts!"

Cab, Tram, and Motorcar

Sled. 1900s

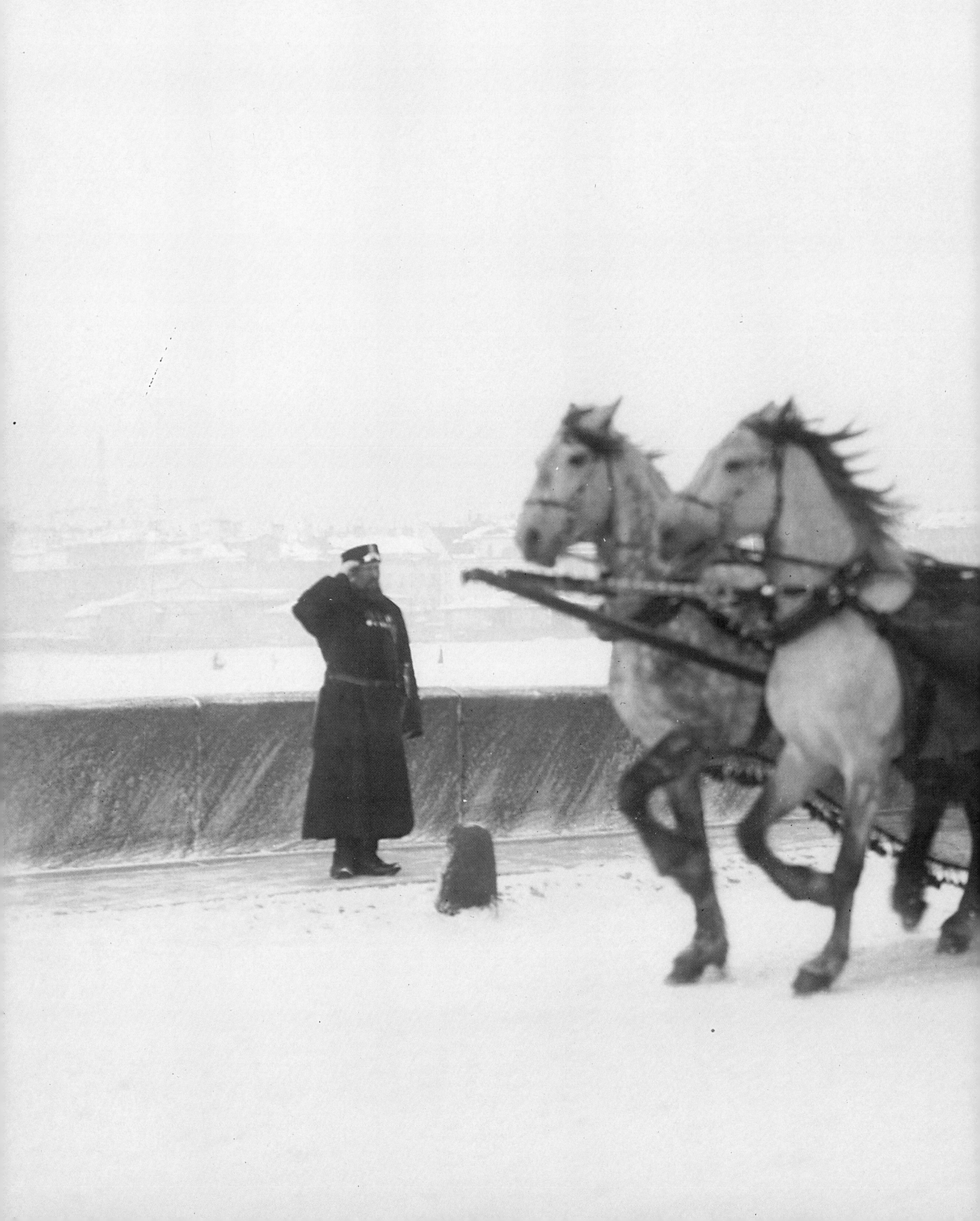

French Renault cars in Palace Square. 1910s

Bus inspection. 1910–12

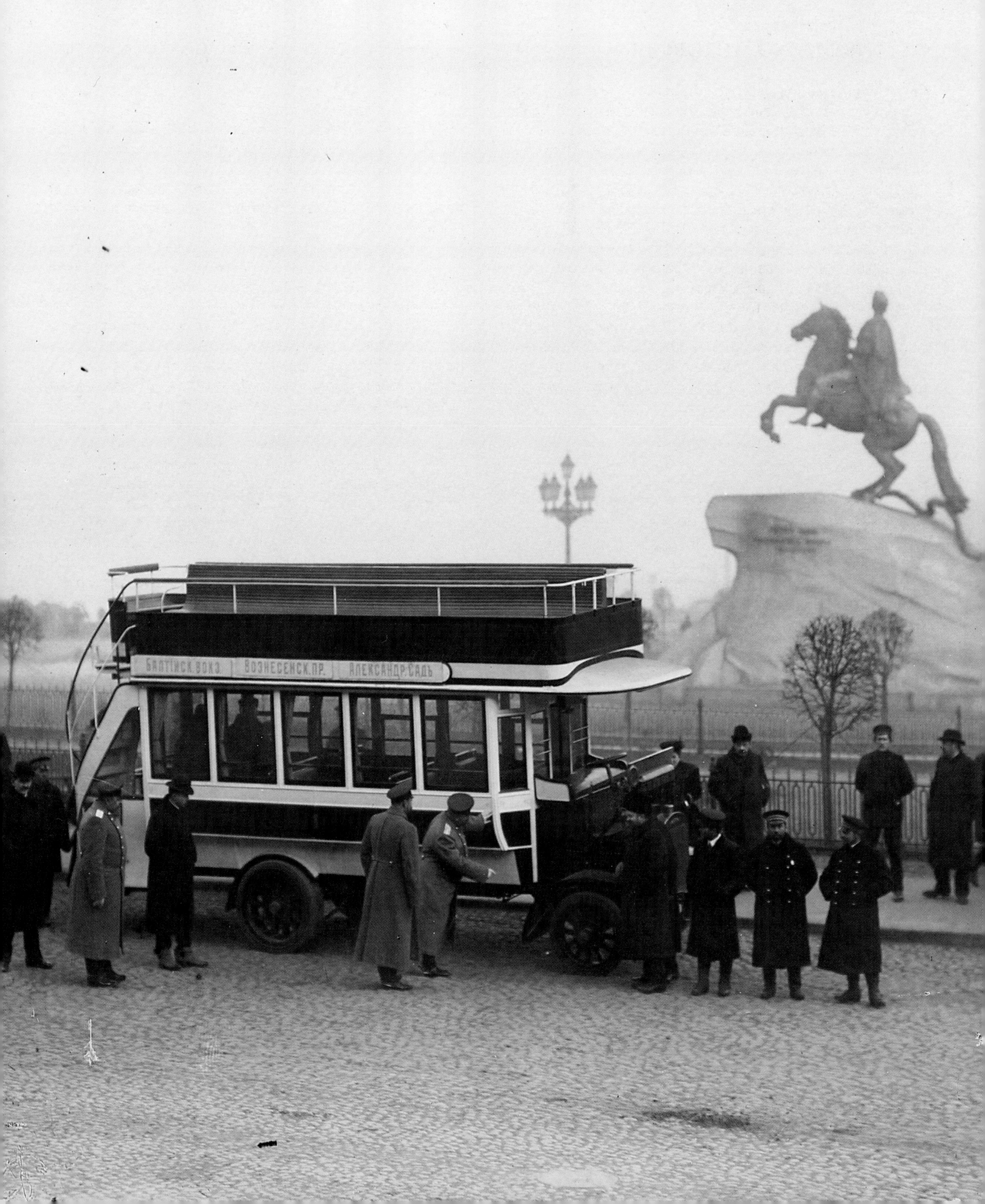

CAB, TRAM, AND MOTORCAR

Contemporaries attest that a new arrival to St. Petersburg who emerged on a station square had his nostrils assaulted by the stench of horse dung. It seemed to saturate the air and seep into the wooden structures and all the cracks and crevices in the stone buildings and pavements. For two centuries the horse in Petersburg was a permanent feature of the landscape, and its presence enlivened the broad thoroughfares and the filthy courtyards in Petersburg's outskirts. In 1900 the number of carters amounted to 26,485; by 1913 that number had doubled. More than 200,000 wheels rumbled over the cobblestone pavements day and night. As Lev Uspensky recalled, every day you could see "tens of thousands of trotters, horses, jades, thoroughbred colts." Catering to the huge horse fleet was a whole industry that bought and sold large quantities of oats and hay, mended harnesses, carts, and carriages, and shod horses; it included numerous veterinaries, horse auctions, riding grounds, indoor courses and hippodromes, and stables; and, of course, there were always horse thieves.

As the population and the size of the city grew, transport became a problem. In 1847 the first omnibus started running along the main Petersburg thoroughfare, from the Admiralty to Znamenskaya Square. It was popularly nicknamed "Forty martyrs" because of the number of passengers it could carry and, presumably, the discomfort of their ride. Four years later, omnibus carriages painted in various colors were running on four permanent routes. Communication between the capital and its suburbs was facilitated by coaches, which took passengers from Gostiny Dvor to Peterhof and the Alexandrovskoye Village.

A decade and a half later, the Joint Stock Society of Horse Railways introduced a horse-drawn tram called the *konka*, a word that quickly became part of the everyday vocabulary of the citizens. The first tram track was laid along Nevsky Prospekt. Very soon the cheap and generally affordable means of transportation won the hearts not only of Petersburg's children, but also of staid old-timers. By 1877 the center of the city was crisscrossed by 26 tram routes with a total length of 84 versts (1 verst = 1.06 km, or 0.66 mile). A ride inside the carriage cost five kopecks, and on the roof, where two benches ran the whole length of the carriage, three kopecks. Varying in size and color, drawn by a single horse in small streets, by two horses in the center, the *konkas* had difficulty crossing crowded intersections and especially climbing the steep, humpbacked bridges over the Neva. For this purpose, horses were usually available on the approaches to a bridge to assist the railcar's climb. After harnessing the horse to the carriage, the boys who manned them sent them galloping, and once the car was over the hump, they detached their horses and returned at a trot.

The first tram, patented by engineer F. A. Piratsky, was tested back in 1880. The new kind of transport did not go into service, however, until September 29 (16 o.s), 1907. Up to then the rail track in Petersburg was the property of the Joint Stock Society of Horse Railways, under an agreement the city council had signed for an imprudently long term. The electric tram, which unexpectedly became a "winter" phenomenon, beginning in 1895, had to make do with tracks laid across the ice-bound Neva. Long before it appeared on city streets, the tram became a popular means of crossing the river.

A new era in the history of the city's transport was ushered in on August 1895. Almost all the capital's newspapers reported the "miracle" that had appeared in Petersburg's streets and had drawn crowds of curious people. It was the first "horseless carriage." The *Birzhevye Vedomosti* wrote that a motorcar could travel at a speed of up to 25 versts an hour, and its tank contained enough fuel for 6 hours of driving. The introduction of "self-propelled carriages" did not pass without incident. The press carried reports of "horses panicking at the sight of them." The monopoly of the horse as the main means of transport was undermined. Although they would still be used along with cars for quite some time yet, they were clearly on the way out.

The futurologists of the nineteenth century, who warned that citizens were in danger of being choked by the stench of horse dung, were mistaken, and they also underestimated the danger of the new transport. Meanwhile, it was constantly being improved, and the design and shape of its models kept changing. By 1913 there were 2,585 cars in St. Petersburg. The general picture of city transport in the early twentieth century was still mixed. Along with the first cars, buses, and trams, one could still see, on the city's squares and embankments, a modest cabby, a smart "road hog," and occasionally an omnibus living out its last days.

One of the first trucks driven by an internal-combustion engine. Early 1900s

OPPOSITE, ABOVE:
A city cabman (*likhach*). 1910s

OPPOSITE, BELOW.
A cabman in a city street. 1910s

ABOVE:
A cabman. 1910s

"One could stop and stand on the sidewalk," wrote Lev Uspensky, "and watch with delight a snorting black or dun horse, breathing steam, like a dragon, out of its twitching nostrils, snow coming up in fountains from under the runs of the sled. Behind the horse sits the cabman in grim concentration."

LEFT:
***Troika*. 1900s**

ABOVE:
Extracting ice from the Neva. 1900s

Water carrier from Okhta. 1907–10
Water carriers were always to be seen in the streets, in summer and winter.
A water main was commissioned in St. Petersburg in 1863 to serve part of the
city center between the Neva and the Obvodny Canal. By 1873 running water
was supplied to Vasilyevsky Island and the Petersburg and Vyborg sides. The
working class outskirts — outside the Nevsky Quarters, Staraya and Novaya
Derevnia (Old and New Villages), Malaya and Bolshaya Okhta, etc. — continued to get their water from wells and from the Neva and its branches.

ABOVE:

Rubbish disposal. 1912

Rubbish disposal was one of the most important utilities. Most of this work was carried out by peasants from the surrounding villages: Ruchyi, Piskariovka, Rogatka, Kolomiagi, Grazhdanka, and others. Most of the men in these villages were cabbies, for whom farming was just a sideline.

RIGHT, ABOVE:

Gathering rags in Nikolsky Market. 1900

RIGHT, BELOW:

Mail being loaded at the St. Petersburg Post Office. Pochtamtskaya Street. 1906

OPPOSITE, ABOVE:

Carters. 1900s

OPPOSITE, BELOW:

Petersburg cabman with a taximeter developed by De Rebert. 1910–12

PRECEDING PAGES:
Omnibus en route. 1906

ABOVE:
Horse-drawn trams in the courtyard of the Joint Stock Society of Horse Railways. 1898

BELOW:
Drivers of the Joint Stock Society of Horse Railways walking their horses. 1898

OPPOSITE, ABOVE:
Horse-drawn tram on the floating Palace Bridge. 1905–06

OPPOSITE, BELOW:
Horse-drawn tram on Anichkov Bridge. 1906

Passengers embarking on a ferry at the Senate Crossing. 1900s

The "laundry" landing pier on the Fontanka. 1910–11
Water transport did much to make up for the shortage of other transportation
and bridges across the rivers and canals. Passenger ships plied the Neva and the
Fontanka regularly from 7 a.m. to 11 p.m. with intervals of 5 to 7 minutes.

Ferryman on a rowboat. 1900

Trams crossing the Neva over ice. 1900s

Crossing the Neva on a sleigh in winter. 1900s

OPPOSITE:

**Steam engine.
Sampsoniyevsky Prospekt.
Early 1900s**

One of the means of public transit in the capital in the early twentieth century was the railway. One line operated in Lesnoye, the other began not far from Znamenskaya Square and reached as far as the village of Murzinki, beyond the Obukhovsky Steel Works. A small locomotive served by an engineer and a fireman pulled *konka*-type cars, some open in summer, others with seats on the roof that were used by passengers who did not mind the smoke, soot, and sparks from the engine.

ABOVE:

Launching of the electric tram. 1907

Opening of tram service in the city. 1907

The ceremony opening the tram service in the capital was held on September 29 (16 o.s.), 1907. It could not take place earlier because of the long-term contract the municipal authorities had signed with the owners of the *konkas*, of horse-drawn trams.

This was how the event was reported by one newspaper: "Shortly after 9 o'clock, invited spectators began to arrive at the Alexandrovsky Gardens, where a huge tent was set up decorated with tropical plants. At the entrance to the gardens tram-drivers in spick-and-span uniforms lined up in two rows. Ten engine trams bedecked with national flags stood on the tracks. Elegant, painted in bright colors and glittering, they drew admiration from the thousands of spectators. . . . Throughout the day the departure of the trams was a big public attraction, and all the trams were packed full of passengers when they left."

OPPOSITE, ABOVE:
Army staff vehicles. 1905

OPPOSITE, BELOW:
Ambulances. 1910s

LEFT, ABOVE:
Motor taxis at the Cathedral of Saints Peter and Paul. 1910
On April 29, 1909, the newspaper *Novoye Vremia* carried this report: "The new society, St. Petersburg Motor Taxi, goes into operation as of May 1 in Petersburg. The fare is 40 kopecks per one verst, one ruble an hour is charged during stops. The motor taxis have no definite ranks and can be hailed and stopped like ordinary cabs in any part of the city. All the taxis are American-made Fords, which are light and elegant. The drivers are dressed in French fashions. By May 1, fifteen motor taxis will be in operation and gradually their number will be brought up to five hundred."

LEFT, BELOW:
The motor fleet of the Central Post Office. 1906

ABOVE:
Fresh from the press: The latest issue of the daily *Birzhevye Vedomosti* is ready to be delivered throughout the city on special motor vehicles. 40 Galernaya Street. 1912

OVERLEAF:
Bus in Vladimirsky Prospekt. 1911

From Alpha to Omega

Dancing lesson at the Smolny Institute for Daughters of the Nobility. 1914

FROM ALPHA TO OMEGA

A country's level of development is often judged by the degree of the emancipation of its women. But perhaps the degree of civilization can be judged just as reliably by the state of people's education, which reflects the state's strengths and weaknesses. Russia, a land of glaring contrasts between wealth and poverty, humility and rebelliousness, revealed a paradoxical combination of European learning and appalling illiteracy. In 1913 many talented scientists, inventors, and engineers who would do credit to any country lived among a population three-fourths of whom could not even sign their name.

Russia had fewer students (3.85 percent of the population) and spent less money on their training than any other European country. Interminable talk about the need for reforming the educational system and expanding the network of schools yielded little. Between 1897 and 1917 the country had a succession of ten education ministers. The activity of the Education Ministry was often described as "people's darkening" (in contrast to "people's enlightenment," as education was referred to in Russia). In January 1905, 342 scientists, including 16 members of the Academy of Sciences and 125 professors, launched an appeal that evoked a broad response in Russia and abroad (it was subsequently signed by 1,500 people). The appeal read in part: "The government's policy in educating the people, guided primarily by police considerations, is a brake on development, stunting the spiritual growth and leading the state into decline."

The character of the military-police state that was the Russian Empire, with strict regulation of every aspect of life, was manifested everywhere. Officers, policemen and gendarmes, clerks, and even students and youthful pupils of gymnasia, or grammar schools, wore identical caps, overcoats, and uniforms. The Table of Ranks, which was adopted in Peter's time and remained valid until the February Revolution of 1917, not only divided society into ranks but also ascribed to everyone his place in accordance with his estate. It affected the educational system, too. The Law School and the Alexandrovsky Lyceum, the Oriental Languages School at the Ministry of Foreign Affairs, the Cadet Corps, and the Smolny Institute for young ladies were open only to children of noble birth, who also enjoyed preferential treatment in the Pavlovsky and Kseniinsky institutes. Children of the gentry accounted for more than half of all pupils in male gymnasia. The children of the urban poor could hope for at best an elementary education. As of 1913 80 percent of adolescents did not attend school.

At that time more than seventy thousand Petersburg children studied at seven hundred elementary schools and classes. However, St. Petersburg was far behind European capitals and behind Moscow as to the level of elementary education (three years long compared with four years in Moscow schools). Higher education in Russia presented a motley picture with schools of every description. There were about thirty types of general education schools. In addition, Petersburg had fifty-three trade schools, thirteen vocational schools and instructional workshops, thirteen

medical schools and courses, one electrical engineering and one telegraph school, a brewery school, maritime schools, private driving schools, not to speak of numerous single courses — tailoring and sewing, stenography, typing, bookkeeping, etc. Their number varied, but on the eve of World War I, they catered to about twenty thousand students.

Traditional humanities education in the classical mold was offered by thirty-six gymnasia in Petersburg. Their graduates had enormous opportunities. The challenges of industrial growth, which required more specialized training, doubled the number of students (from twenty-four to forty-eight thousand) in the first decade of the 1900s. Among the eighty-odd male secondary schools, twenty were grammar schools and more than twenty were commercial schools. Children of poor parents had little chance of entering these schools, however. The tuition there was 200–250 rubles a year (which was often more than the annual income of a factory worker). This compared with 80 rubles in ordinary secondary schools. It must be said in fairness that bright children from low-income families were exempt from paying tuition if their academic performance was good.

There was little coeducation in tsarist Russia; the government quashed such proposals from pedagogical congresses. In Petersburg there were only the Vyborg Commercial School, a few dozen elementary schools, and two or three private schools offering instruction to both sexes. As a result, there was a flourishing system of women's education. At the start of the twentieth century, women accounted for more than half the capital's inhabitants with a secondary education.

As a result of the prolonged struggle by progressives for women's equality, many higher schools for women sprang up in the late nineteenth century. In 1895 M. A. Lokhvitskaya-Skalon opened a modern-language course. In 1896 courses for women physical-training instructors were opened by P. F. Lesshaft. The following year the Women's Medical Institute was opened. It was one of the best educational establishments in the capital. At the beginning of the twentieth century, three-year Higher Women's Courses in Natural Sciences and Agronomy were opened by Professor Stebut. But top among the women's schools was the Bestuzhev Higher Courses, whose curricula approximated that of universities. It had over five thousand students by the 1910s. At about the same time women began to attend universities and institutes on a free basis.

Higher educational establishments were mushrooming in Petersburg. Their number increased from twenty-one in 1895 to sixty in 1914. Along with traditional scientific and educational centers of long standing, such as the University; the Mining, Forestry, and Technological institutes, institutes of communications and civil engineering; the Military Medical Academy; the Academy of Arts; the Conservatoire; and the Religious Academy, there appeared the Electrical Engineering, Polytechnic, and many other institutes. Although the number of places at these establishments was large (more than seven thousand at the University, about five thousand at the Polytechnic, about two thousand each at the Technological and Mining institutes), the number of applicants every year far outnumbered vacancies, which led to tough compe-

The Universitetskaya (University) Embankment. Academy of Sciences (with columns) and the Kunstkammer (with tower). Early 1900s

Students of the Religious (Greek Orthodox) Academy. December 28 (15 o.s.), 1909
In the early twentieth century there were several religious schools in Petersburg: two academies, two seminaries (Orthodox and Roman Catholic), and an Orthodox religious school.

tition. For instance, in the early 1900s there were seven hundred applicants for the fifty places open at the Mining Institute, and facilities at the higher-education institutions varied in quality as the institutes operated under various government departments. By and large, their equipment was better than that at the Acade-my of Sciences laboratories, and so many major scientists and specialists preferred to work at institutes and universities, pursuing research and at the same time training their successors. Petersburg produced many scientists of world renown, such as Dmitry Mendeleyev, Ivan Pavlov, and Vladimir Vernadsky.

Children and their parents lining up to enroll at the City People's School. 52, 7th Line, Vasilyevsky Island. 1913

ABOVE:
Coeducation school of the Alexander Nevsky Temperance Society. 1909

CENTER:
A class for young children at Nicholas I's Institute for Orphans. 1900s

LEFT:
Children from a nursery of the Expedition for the Manufacture of Government Papers. 144 Fontanka Embankment. 1903

241

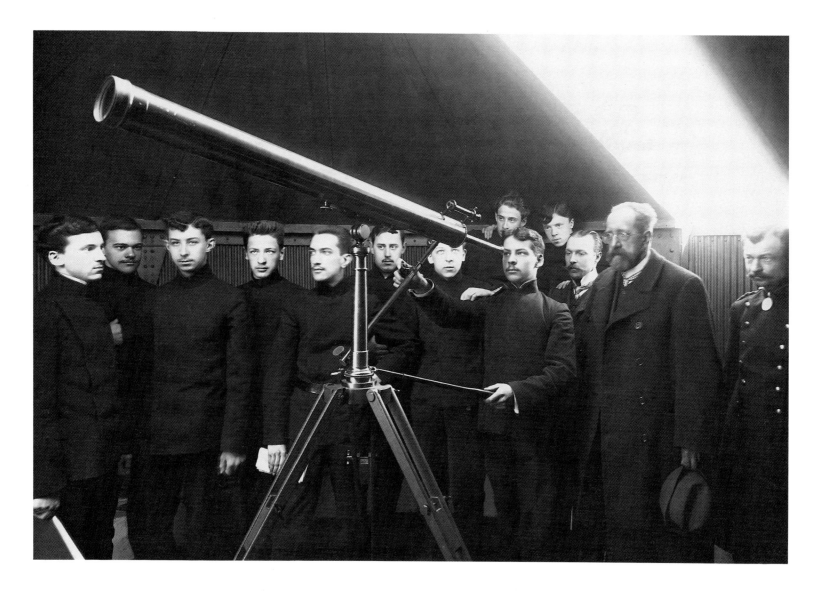

OPPOSITE, ABOVE:
Pupils of the Petrovskoye School (run by the Merchants Society) at the school's observatory. 1908

OPPOSITE, BELOW:
Students at the Peter the Great Gymnasium with their teacher. Bolshoi Prospekt, Petersburg Side. 1900

A group of students of the Imperial Alexandrovsky Lyceum in a garden near the bust of Alexander Pushkin. 1911

Many famous people came out of the Lyceum at Tsarskoye Selo. The first graduation included especially remarkable public men, poets, and artists, the most famous being Pushkin himself. Among the others were the Decembrists Ivan Pushchin and Wilhelm von Küchelbecker, the poet and publisher Baron Anton Delwig, the famous diplomat and State Chancellor of the Empire Prince Alexander Gorchakov, the tireless traveler Admiral Fiodor Matiushkin, and others. In 1843 the Lyceum was moved from Tsarskoye Selo to the premises of the former Alexandrovsky House for Orphans on the Petersburg Side. However, the early "Lyceum spirit" did not survive 1822, when the Lyceum was put under the Department of Military Education Institutions. Pushkin lamented the change:

Fate with its iron hand
Smote our peaceful Lyceum.

243

Naval Cadet Corps on parade to mark the centenary of the Battle of Borodino. Palace Square. 1912

The Cadet Corps were exclusive secondary educational establishments for children of hereditary noblemen or officers — who thereby acquired for themselves the status of nobility — children of the clergy, Cossacks, and pupils from Slavic countries of the same station. In 1911–14 the country had twenty-six Cadet Corps with a student body of more than ten thousand. There were six corps in Petersburg, including junior classes of the Page Corps and the Naval Cadet Corps.

Military band of the Pavlovskoye Cadet School. 1913

At the end of the nineteenth century Russia had ten schools for cadets with a two-year term of study. In 1903 the term of study was increased to three years, and the schools had about ten thousand graduates annually. There were eight military schools in Petersburg: the Corps of the Pages, two infantry schools, two artillery schools, a cavalry school, and an engineering and a topographic school; and six armed-forces academies: military, naval, artillery, engineering, military-medical, military legal, and, from 1911, the Quartermaster School.

Lesson in fire fighting at the Fire Technicians Courses.
St. Petersburg City Public Authority. 1910

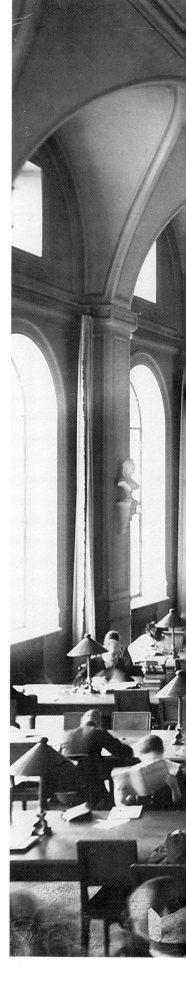

ABOVE:

The building of the Imperial Polytechnic Institute. 1–3 Lesnoi Prospekt, the "Road to Sosnovka." 1907

RIGHT:

The building of the Women's Medical Institute. 8 Arkhiyereiskaya Street. 1913

BELOW:

Building of the Imperial Public Library. 1910s

The Public Library, founded in Petersburg in 1795, was formally opened two decades later, on January 14 (2 o.s.), 1814. Its director was Alexei Olenin, writer, scientist, and art lover. Over the years its staff members included Nikolai Gnedich, poet and translator of the *Iliad*; Ivan Krylov, writer of fables; Anton Delwig, Pushkin's Lyceum friend; poet Konstantin Batiushkov; writer Mikhail Zagoskin; music and art critic Vladimir Stasov; and many others. Among the famous public men, cultural figures and scholars who frequented the library were Vissarion Belinsky, Nikolai Chernyshevsky, Count Leo Tolstoy, Georgy Plekhanov, Maxim Gorky, and Lenin.

OPPOSITE:

The main reading hall at the Imperial Public Library. 1910

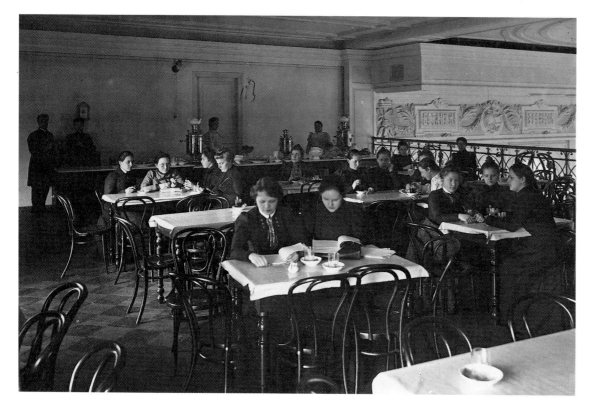

ABOVE:
**Students, teachers, and guests on the day of the centenary of the
Institute of Communications Engineers, named after Emperor
Alexander I. 1910**

**Students of the Bestuzhev Higher Courses for Women in a dining
room. 1900**

**Students and lecture-goers at the Imperial St. Petersburg
University in the dining room. 1910**

Dmitry Ivanovich Mendeleyev, chemist, the creator of the periodic table of chemical elements; founder and first director of the Chamber of Measures and Weights. 1890s

Anatoly Fiodorovich Koni, lawyer and public figure, member of the State Council, writer, and honorary member of the St. Petersburg Academy of Sciences. 1910s

In 1878 Koni, then chairman of the St. Petersburg District Court, presided over a cause célèbre, the trial of Vera Zasulich, who made an attempt on the life of General Fiodor Trepov, the administrative "mayor" of Petersburg noted for his cruel treatment of political prisoners. Zasulich was acquitted by a jury verdict upheld by the judge. Alexander II asked Koni for his immediate resignation, but he firmly refused, suggesting the sovereign oust him instead, or otherwise confirm the newly established law concerning the independence and life-long tenure of the judges. The liberal tsar chose to comply with the law. Recalling that episode, Koni wrote: "Fortune ordained that I should remain a loyal servant of the principles to which I have been committed since my time at the University, and the friendship and respect of such people as Kavelin and Granovsky, Artsimovich, Count Miliutin, Chicherin, and Count L. N. Tolstoy more than compensated for the corrupting benevolence of august personalities and their treacherous and ingratiating 'counsels and army men'."

RIGHT:

Nikolai Petrovich Likhachov, historian, member of the Academy of Sciences, founder of the Paleography Museum. 1910s

ABOVE:

Ivan Petrovich Pavlov, physiologist, with a group of students at a lecture. 1907–08

OPPOSITE:

Vladimir Mikhailovich Bekhterev, founder and head of the Psychoneurological Institute, at a hypnosis session. 1913

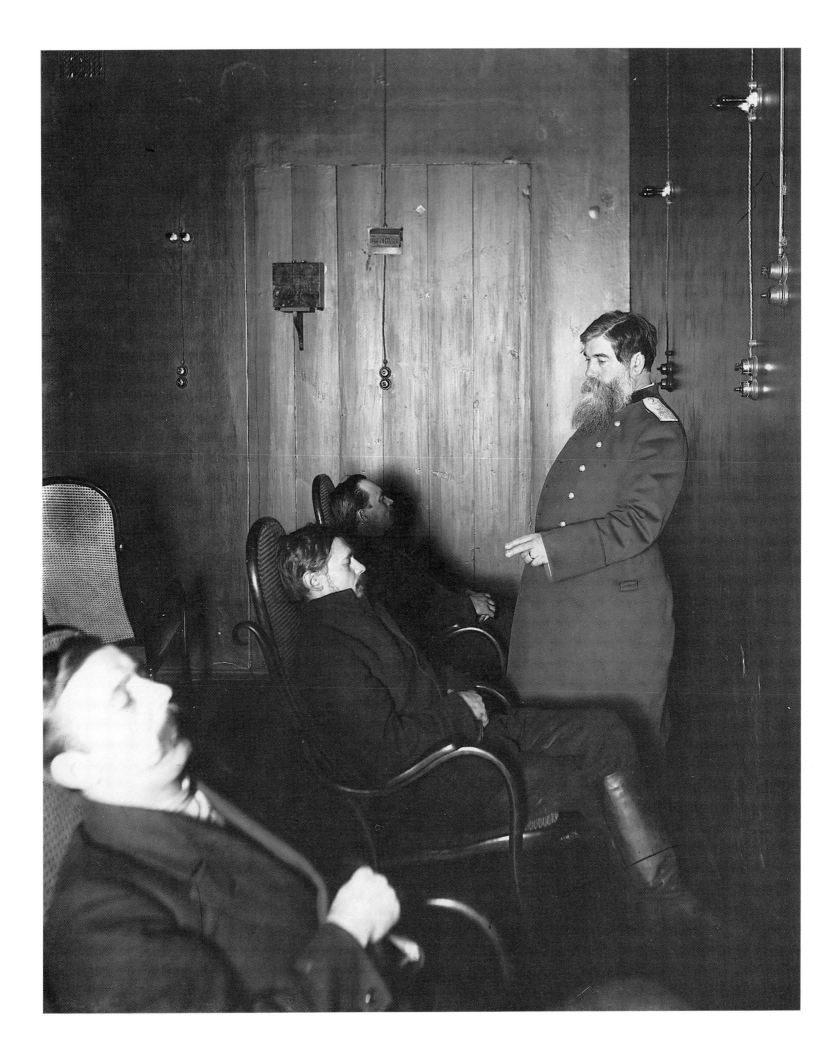

ABOVE:

Stepan Osipovich Makarov, Russian naval commander, vice-admiral, and oceanographer. 1896

The icebreaker *Ermak*. Early 1900s

The world's first icebreaker capable of crushing 1-meter-thick ice was named after Ermak Timofeyevich, a Cossack commander whose expedition started the colonization of Siberia in 1589. The icebreaker, the brainchild of vice-admiral Stepan Makarov, was built in Britain in 1899 under his supervision. Heavy Arctic ice was more than a match for the icebreaker; it was used instead in the Baltic at the Kronstadt port.

Arts and Feasts

**Monument to Mikhail Glinka. Teatralnaya (Theater) Square.
1910–13**

Exposition of the Imperial Agricultural Museum.
1 Rynochnaya Street. 1900s

Sestroretsk, a holiday resort on the Gulf of Finland. 1913

ARTS AND FEASTS

In the middle of the nineteenth century, enlightened Europe, spoiled by an abundance of fine arts and long having breathed the air of the Renaissance, left behind the elation and elegance of the Baroque, the sumptuous Rococo and Empire styles, the monumental conventions of Neo-Classicism, the Sturm und Drang of the Romantics, and embarked on a new phase in the development of human culture and civilization. Weary of elegance and diversity of forms, genres, and trends, aesthetically sophisticated and blasé, Europe was stunned by the flowering of Russian culture, which rediscovered long-forgotten values and discovered new ones, and presented an astonishingly novel vision of man and the diversity of the historical, natural, and spiritual landscape.

With its roots going back to the traditions of the early chronicles and the remarkable *Song of Igor's Campaign*, a literary monument of Old Rus, Russian culture drew on the treasure house of folklore — legends, songs, *bylinas* (folk epics), myths, Slavic learning and Byzantine scholarship, the unique and magnificent St. Sophia cathedrals in Kiev and Novgorod, the austere and spiritually exalted frescoes and icons of Andrei Rublev, the spiritual quests of the *startsi* (unordained and ordained priests) to the east of the Volga River, and the inspired writings and messages of the "fiery" Archpriest Avvakum. Over the ages it became imbued with the beauty of Russian nature, which seems tranquil and somewhat subdued at first sight, but on closer inspection reveals a multitude of shades and half-tones, which form a unique picture.

Russian art had been slowly building up its treasure trove over the centuries, adding brilliant works and drawing generously from the wellspring of European and world culture. But in the nineteenth century it exploded, producing a galaxy of outstanding men of letters, artists, and musicians, who added a unique page to the history of Russian and world culture. Spearheading that outburst of creativity was Russian literature. The novelists Ivan Turgenev, Fiodor Dostoyevsky, and Leo Tolstoy, who were the first to gain a worldwide audience for Russian literature, discovered something more than just the unknown Russian land. They discovered the new and authentically original inner world of their heroes: spontaneous, sensitive, and perceptive not only of the surrounding life, but of the movements of their own souls.

"Not enough sun — this is the clue to Russian history. Long nights explain Russian obsession with psychology." This ironic but penetrating remark was made by the writer Vasily Rozanov in the early twentieth century. The absence of democratic freedoms in Russia, which made it impossible to discuss openly urgent social and political issues, channeled social thought into literary forms. It fell to Russian writers — with their lofty spirituality, inner freedom, and independence, their quests and outspoken judgments and views, their exposure to universal humanistic experience — to fill the vacuum, in which according to Alexander Herzen, not only village and village, but thought and thought were thousands of miles apart. Perhaps from Pushkin and Gogol from whom, according to Dostoyevsky, the whole of Russian literature originated, there persisted the great tradition of charity and compassion for the "little man," defenseless in the face of a hostile government bureaucracy, weak in the face of the reigning powers, suffering and needing help; the great tradition of love and respect of the people. The peculiarly Russian phenomenon of the "intelligentsia" owes much to that tradition.

Literature occupied a special place in Russia's spiritual life. Writers exerted an enormous influence on public consciousness. Dostoyevsky, who died in 1881, was the most prophetic of nineteenth-centurty writers, producing works comparable in magnitude to those of Shakespeare and Rembrandt. Having revealed the innermost and darkest recesses of the human soul, exposed its good and evil sides, he declared his famous motto: "Be humble, proud man! Not given his due and not fully understood by his contemporaries, the author of *The Idiot*, *The Possessed*, and *The Brothers Karamazov* invariably stirred thought and human conscience, provoking heated arguments and conflicting opinions. Many major twentieth-century writers in Russia and abroad acknowledged their debt to him.

Until his death in 1910, the brightest star in the literary firmament had been Count Leo Tolstoy, of whom the journalist and publisher Alexei Suvorin said in the early twentieth century: "We have two tsars: Nicholas II and Leo Tolstoy. Who is the stronger? Nicholas II can do nothing to Tolstoy, he cannot shake his throne, while Tolstoy undoubtedly is shaking the throne of Nicholas II and his dynasty... . If anyone touches Tolstoy, the whole world will scream." According to a 1905 poll of Petersburg students, 39 percent believed the greatest formative influence on them had been exerted by Leo Tolstoy, who by that time had been anathematized and excommunicated from the Russian Orthodox Church by the Holy Synod.

The whole Realist tradition of Russian literature of the late nineteenth and early twentieth centuries was influenced by Dostoyevsky and Tolstoy. Among its brilliant representatives were Anton Chekhov, Vladimir Korolenko, Dmitry Grigorovich, Alexander Kuprin, Gleb Uspensky, Vikenty Veresayev, and Ivan Bunin.

As in the West, art in Russia, especially in Petersburg, saw along with Realism the rise of other modernist trends, which thrived on a new perception of the world, a troubled and anxious view of human consciousness that became increasingly volatile and morbid under the influence of rapid change. "The searing years," as the Russian poet Alexander Blok described them, left an imprint on several generations who considered themselves the children of "Russia's terrible years." Drawing on the philosophical and ethical works of Vladimir Solovyov, Nikolai Berdiayev, and Vasily Rozanov, artistic thought conquered new summits and looked for new forms. It was at the same time attracted and repelled by analogues in Russia and in Europe in its search for an identity. New ideas were powerfully expressed in the works of Valery Briusov, Konstantin Balmont, Alexander Blok, Andrei Bely (pen name of Boris Bugayev), Anna Akhmatova, Fiodor Sologub (pen name of Fiodor Teternikov), Zinaida Gippius, Dmitry Merezhkovsky, Viacheslav Ivanov, and many others.

At the same time, Maxim Gorky, who had converted many to

the revolutionary cause, brought together new proletarian writers who continued the tradition of the Revolutionary Democrats. The "Muse of Revenge and Grief," which inspired these writers and poets, and the "Beautiful Lady," or "Sophia," the symbol of modernist poetry, walked the same Petersburg streets and even called at the same houses, usually shunning each other, but sometimes being forced to engage in acrimonious debate. These two trends in art conducted their own parts in the literary process as in a Bach fugue.

Artists who shared aesthetic and social views rallied around periodicals, which, in the context of sharpening political struggles, sought to formulate their literary and social views with utter clarity. In addition to long-established major publishing houses of Suvorin, Marx, and Stasiulevich, Petersburg's cultural life was vividly represented in the latest publications such as the *World of Art* (*Mir Iskusstva*), *New Life* (*Novaya Zhizn*), *New Way* (*Novy Put*), and *Knowledge* (*Znaniye*).

The Russian book market, one of the smallest in the world as late as the 1880s, was swamped by a mounting flood of books and periodicals, which inundated the Russian capital in the early twentieth century. One in every four Russian periodicals (472 newspapers and magazines as of 1910) and nearly one-quarter of all books were published in Petersburg. Bookshops and bookstalls occupied almost the whole of Liteiny and Vladimirsky Prospekts and Simeonovskaya Street, impressing visitors with a dazzling diversity of books, magazines, albums, and prints, both antique and modern.

At the turn of the century the tradition of intimate spiritual communication, of soirées and salons with their interminable arguments about art and life, music and poetry recitals, and theatrical shows — far from outliving itself — was just as widespread and popular as it had been a century earlier. Some of the more remarkable literary and theatrical evenings in early twentieth-century Petersburg were held in Viacheslav Ivanov's "tower" at the corner of Tavricheskaya and Tverskaya streets; a select society gathered at the salon of Zinaida Gippius and Dmitry Merezhkovsky in the house of Prince Muruzi on Liteiny Prospekt. Young poets flocked to Fiodor Sologub's "Areopagus";

later he held "Thursdays" in his flat in Razyezzhaya Street, which attracted the cream of Petersburg's writers and artists. An indispensable part of these occasions were fancy dress balls and intellectual disputes. They were frequented by Leonid Andreyev, Alexei Tolstoy, Anna Akhmatova, the actresses Larisa Yavorskaya, Elizaveta Time, and Vera Yureneva. It was here that Igor Severianin made his debut. Alexander Blok was an occasional visitor. Many outstanding scientists and artists, including Vladimir Stasov, Fiodor Chaliapin, Dmitry Mendeleyev, Vladimir Korolenko, Ivan Pavlov, Vladimir Bekhterev, Vladimir Mayakovsky, Maxim Gorky, and Isaak Brodsky, gathered at "Repin Wednesdays" in Penaty, in the village of Kuokkala on the Gulf of Finland. On Saturdays the great actress Vera Komissarzhevskaya who had left the official stage and founded her own theater at the Passage in 1904, held her salon.

By the beginning of the twentieth century dramatic changes had taken place in the theater. After an upsurge in the mid-century which owed much to the remarkable dramatist Alexander Ostrovsky, Russian theater increased its repertoire by adding many Russian plays. From the early twentieth century its development was associated with the name of Anton Chekhov who, together with the outstanding stage director Konstantin Stanislavsky, managed to change the whole course of modern dramatic thinking.

The search for new ways in art produced a crop of new theaters. Alongside the long-famous Mariinsky and Alexandrinka theaters, appeared the new theaters of Konmissarzhevskaya, the Novy Theatre (New Theatre) opened by the actress Larisa Yavorskaya, the Maly Theatre of Alexei Suvorin, the Starinny Theatre (Ancient Theatre), which was opened and closed twice, the Modern Theatre, and the private theater of K.N. Nezlobin. The Russian Drama Theatre of A.K. Reineke was housed in the premises of the Panayev Theatre. A number of miniature theaters sprang up: the Troitsky, Liteiny, Intimny, The Crooked Mirror, and others. The People's House of Emperor Nicholas II on the Petersburg Side and the People's House of Countess Panina on Ligovskaya Street also offered their halls for theatrical performances.

The theatrical life of Petersburg was inseparable from musical art, which flourished in Russia, especially due to the efforts of Mikhail Glinka. That tradition continued in the work of the next generation of composers, notably "the mighty handful" — Mily Balakirev, Alexander Borodin, Modest Musorgsky, and Nikolai Rimsky-Korsakov. In the late nineteenth and early twentieth centuries, the Russian musical tradition was taken up and developed by a group of brilliant and highly individual composers and musicians, such as Anton Rubinstein, Alexander Glazunov, Anatoly Liadov, Sergei Rachmaninov, Alexander Scriabin, Igor Stravinsky, Anton Arensky, Nikolai Miaskovsky, Sergei Prokofiev, and Boris Asafyev.

Russian ballet, which was part of the musical process, became preeminent at the turn of the century. Much of the credit for this belongs to Piotr Ilyich Tchaikovsky, the great composer of symphonies who narrowed the gap between ballet and symphony and invested his ballets with drama and psychological depth. His *Sleeping Beauty*, *The Nutcracker*, and *Swan Lake* are gems of world ballet. Glazunov carried on Tchaikovsky's tradition and devoted much of his talent to creating such classic ballets as *Raimonda*, *Temptation of Damis*, and *The Seasons*, which were produced on the famous Mariinsky stage by Marius Petipa, who also staged Tchaikovsky's ballets. In the early twentieth century that remarkable generation of choreographers was replaced by new names. In 1901 Lev Ivanov, one of the most talented ballet masters, died. In 1903 Marius Petipa left the theater after fifty-six years at the head of the brilliant ballet. They had worthy successors in Alexander Gorsky and Michel Fokine, graduates of the Petersburg Theatre School (a ballet school). They were often applauded by ecstatic crowds. But the biggest applause was reserved for the ballet stars Mathilda Kshesinskaya, Olga Preobrazhenskaya, Vera Trefilova, Anna Pavlova, Tamara Karsavina, and many others.

Theater, especially ballet, loomed large in the life and multifarious activities of Sergei Diaghilev, one of the leaders of The World of Art association of artists and organizer of the famous "Russian seasons" in Paris and other European capitals. Since the hugely successful first Ballet Russe season in 1909, ballet dominated Diaghilev's enterprise. Not only did he promote Russian ballet stars, but he also managed to enlist the support of many musicians, artists, and writers. The Russian stage, too, was always open for foreign performers. Many world-famous artists, especially opera singers and musicians, performed in Petersburg.

St. Petersburg, where all the muses seemed to be gathered, was a magnet for the best creative artists of Russia. Actors, musicians, composers, writers, poets, and painters flocked to the city, which was itself a masterpiece and which practically breathed art. Hundreds of talented painters, whose canvases now hang in museums around the world, were trained at the famous Russian Academy of Arts. It was here that the democratic tradition of traveling exhibitions of Realist paintings — of the Wanderers — originated. It was here that new societies and associations of artists were formed that rejected the ossified classical tradition. Among the artists who worked in Petersburg were Ivan Shishkin, Nikolai Yaroshenko, Grigory Miasoyedov, Vladimir Makovsky, Arkhip Kuinji, Ilya Repin, Igor Grabar, Ivan Bilibin, Anna Ostroumova-Lebedeva, Boris Kustodiev, Isaak Brodsky, Nicholas Roerich, Alexander Benois, Leon Bakst, Konstantin Somov, Evgeny Lanceray, and Mstislav Dobuzhinsky.

In an atmosphere of universal interest in art, the Museum of Russian Art named after Emperor Alexander III was opened at the Mikhailovsky Palace on March 7, 1898. (It is now called the Russian Museum.) All in all, there were forty-eight museums in Petersburg at the time, the most popular of which was the Hermitage, with its rich collection of Western European and ancient art, the Zoological Museum (adored by children), the naval, mining, agricultural, and other museums, and numerous temporary exhibitions.

No picture of Petersburg's cultural life would be complete without mentioning the popular feasts that had a long tradition and were much loved by city dwellers (85 percent of whom came from the peasantry and the lower middle class, or *meshchane*). These feasts, first held in Admiralty Square and later in the Field of Mars, attracted as many as sixty to seventy thousand adults and children. "From the Chain Bridge and even from Panteleimonovskaya Street," wrote Dobuzhinsky in his memoirs, "one could hear the cheerful hubbub of human voices in the crisp, frosty air and a whole sea of sounds — hooting, whistling, the monotonous barrel organ, the accordion, tambourines. All this was so exciting that I begged my nanny to take me there as quickly as possible. Fairground booths loomed behind the bare trees of the Summer Garden. These were tall, yellow clapboard barracks stretching in two rows along the whole Field of Mars

People's House of Emperor Nicholas II. Petersburg Side, Alexandrovsky Public Gardens. 1913
The People's House was a huge stone building. On the park side it was surrounded by a terrace, which had pavilions with open stages, tearooms, and kitchens. Operas starring Fiodor Chaliapin and Vitaly Sobinov were performed at Opera Hall. On open stages and little platforms pantomimes, trained animals, magicians, and acrobats could be seen.

with tricolor flags fluttering over each one. Beyond the booths were merry-go-rounds and ice hills, also with flags on top." In 1897, because of overcrowding and the litter that these feasts left in the city squares, they were moved from the center, first to the Preobrazhensky, and a year later, to the Semionovsky Parade Ground. On Shrovetide and on Easter there were popular shows and such attractions as the "American Hills" (switchback) or the "Transvaal Ice Fortress," farce shows, merry-go-rounds, shooting galleries, stalls, and caged animals.

Along with these popular entertainments, leisure increasingly became associated with sports. A skating rink for the élite was opened at the Tavrichesky Garden in the late 1850s. Shortly afterward the first public skating rink was opened in the Yusupovsky Garden in Sadovaya Street. Prince Vladimir Meshchersky wrote about the new fad: "Old men and women, grown-ups and children alike, all developed a craze for buying skates, putting them on, racing to the Tavrichesky Garden, falling down twenty times a minute, etc." Regular championships in speed skating (held since 1889) and national figure-skating contests (held since 1897) where the first Russian Olympic champion, Nikolai Panin-Kolomenkin, shone did much to popularize skating among the citizens and to prepare the birth of a new sport, ice hockey.

Leisure-time activities were greatly influenced by the technological progress sweeping Russia. "Living pictures," the wonderful invention of the French and the Americans, were first shown at Petersburg's Aquarium Garden in May 1896. At that time no one suspected that the cinema would soon conquer the whole world and challenge the theater. Cinemas were springing up all over Petersburg. Within several years there were few streets that did not have glittering lights inviting people to see the comedies of Max Linder or dramas with Francesco Bartini. Scary and tantalizing films such as *The Naked Mistress, In the Seducer's Arms, In the Villain's Grip* took audiences away from the idols of yesteryear, circus wrestlers and sword swallowers.

Horse riding, popular among the rich, was gradually replaced by faster modes of transport — the bicycle and the motorcar. Leather leggings and goggles were the most prestigious accessories of a modern young man. Before long, horse races, which provoked emotions rivaled only by the passions that raged in gambling houses and casinos, gave way to daredevil air pilots who capitured people's hearts and minds.

Lev Uspensky thus described the day of May 4 (April 21 o.s.), 1910, when he waited for the flight of an airplane on the Kolomiazhsky Hippodrome: "Whether there were 100,000 or 80,000 of us I do not know. But we all said in one voice: 'It flies, my God, it flies!' This lasted a few seconds, not longer than one or two minutes, for the forces of nature prevailed over human genius — for the time being.

"In a twinkling the barriers and the police were swept aside. Tens of thousands of people, roaring with delight, overran the guards and raced over the wet spring grass drawing into their yelling and applauding en masse the ground crew, a handful of Frenchmen, Russian members of the air club, overdressed ladies, pickpockets who had a field day relieving the public of their purses, sleuths, food vendors — they were all heading toward the place where M. Hubert Latam, still not quite understanding why they were all running toward him, was popping in and out of his little aircraft that looked rather like a little bathtub or a gondola."

Although many flights of aircraft and air balloons ended tragically and newspapers reported missing sailors and travelers, people were impatient and avid for new conquests and triumphs. No political conflict or social upheaval, no sense of foreboding or imminent catastrophe, can arrest life or check man in his spirited quest for the future.

ABOVE:

The poet Alexander Alexandrovich Blok. Early 1900s

"His genius, which had the breadth and might of Pushkin's harmony, encompassed all the conceivable possibilities of Russian poetry, for a whole decade his voice was the most powerful in it." *Tizian Tabidze*

OPPOSITE:

The future writer Vladimir Nabokov with his mother, Elena Ivanovna. 1908

"I would moreover submit that, in regard to the power of hoarding up impressions, Russian children of my generation passed through a period of genius, as if destiny were loyally trying what it could for them by giving them more than their share, in view of the cataclysm that was to remove completely the world they had known.

"Neither in environment nor in heredity can I find the exact instrument that fashioned me, the anonymous roller that pressed upon my life a certain intricate watermark whose unique design becomes visible when the lamp of art is made to shine through life's foolscap." *Vladimir Nabokov*

The poet Zinaida Gippius; critic and journalist Dmitry Filosofov;
writer, literary scholar, and philosopher Dmitry Merezhkovsky.
1900s

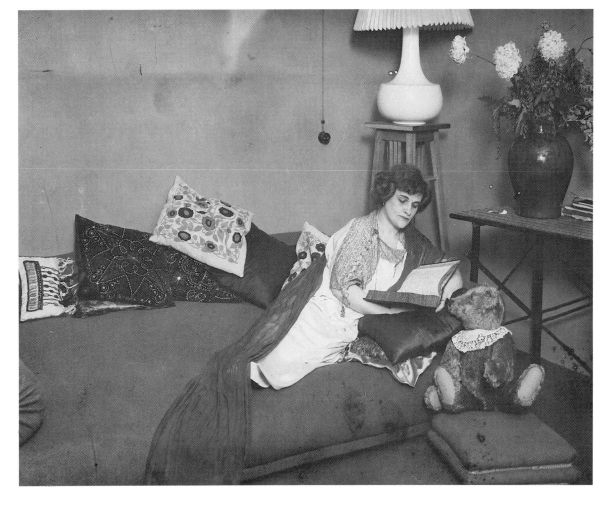

ABOVE:

The writer Fiodor Kuzmich Sologub (Teternikov) with his wife, Anastasia Chebotarevskaya. 1913

"People love to be loved. They like noble and exalted souls. Even in villains they insist on seeing glimmerings of good. . . . That is why they are incredulous when presented with a stark, accurate, dismal and evil picture. They feel like saying: 'He is describing himself.'
'Not so, my dear contemporaries; my novel *The Little Devil* is about you.'
"This novel is a skillfully made mirror. . . . I have measured it many times and checked it thoroughly and it has no curvature. It reflects the ugly and the beautiful with equal precision." *Fiodor Sologub*

The writer Nadezhda Teffi (née Lokhvitskaya, Buchinskaya by marriage). 1900s

World-famous Russian bass Fiodor Chaliapin singing at a performance in a salon of Vladimir Stasov, art and music critic (in the center, sitting). Among his guests are a number of leading figures in Russian culture of the time, Nikolai Rimsky-Korsakov, Alexander Glazunov, Cesar Cui, and Maria Savina to name a few. 1890s

Mathilda Felixovna Kshesinskaya, prima ballerina. 1914

According to the authoritative testimony of Alexander Benois, "in point of skill one couldn't wish for more than what our ballet stage was proud of in this star of the first magnitude. Although Preobrazhenskaya, Trefilova, and Sedova were still and rightly revered by the crowds, Kshesinskaya had a distinctive and brilliant style."

BELOW:

The ballerina Tamara Platonovna Karsavina. Early 1910s

The daughter of a noted Petersburg dancer and teacher, Tamara Karsavina performed at the Mariinsky Theatre in Petersburg from 1902 to 1918 and with Diaghilev's Ballet Russe in the Russian Seasons from 1909 to 1929. She married an Englishman and left Russia in 1918. From 1930 to 1955 she was vice president of the Royal Dance Academy in London. Her partners were the famous Michel Fokine and Vaslav Nijinsky. Alexander Vertinsky, who met her abroad, recalled: "The Germans called her 'Die Karsawina,' 'the Karsavina,' the way they spell the great names only, those that became something more of a phenomenon than of a particular person."

OPPOSITE:

The ballerina Anna Pavlova. Early 1900s

"Anna Pavlova never sought to impress you with her technique," wrote the artist Sergei Makovsky. "She enthralled you with her inspiration. . . . One wanted to feast one's eyes on her, forgetting all the rules of dance, being swept along by the enchantment of her sublime talent."

OPPOSITE:

**The actress Vera Fiodorovna
Komissarzhevskaya. 1900s**
"Komissarzhevskaya is a wonderful
actress," wrote Anton Chekhov in a
letter to Anatoly Koni. "At a rehearsal many wept watching her
and said that she is the best actress
in Russia today."

ABOVE:

**Anastasia Dmitriyevna
Vialtseva, performer of gypsy
songs. 1909**

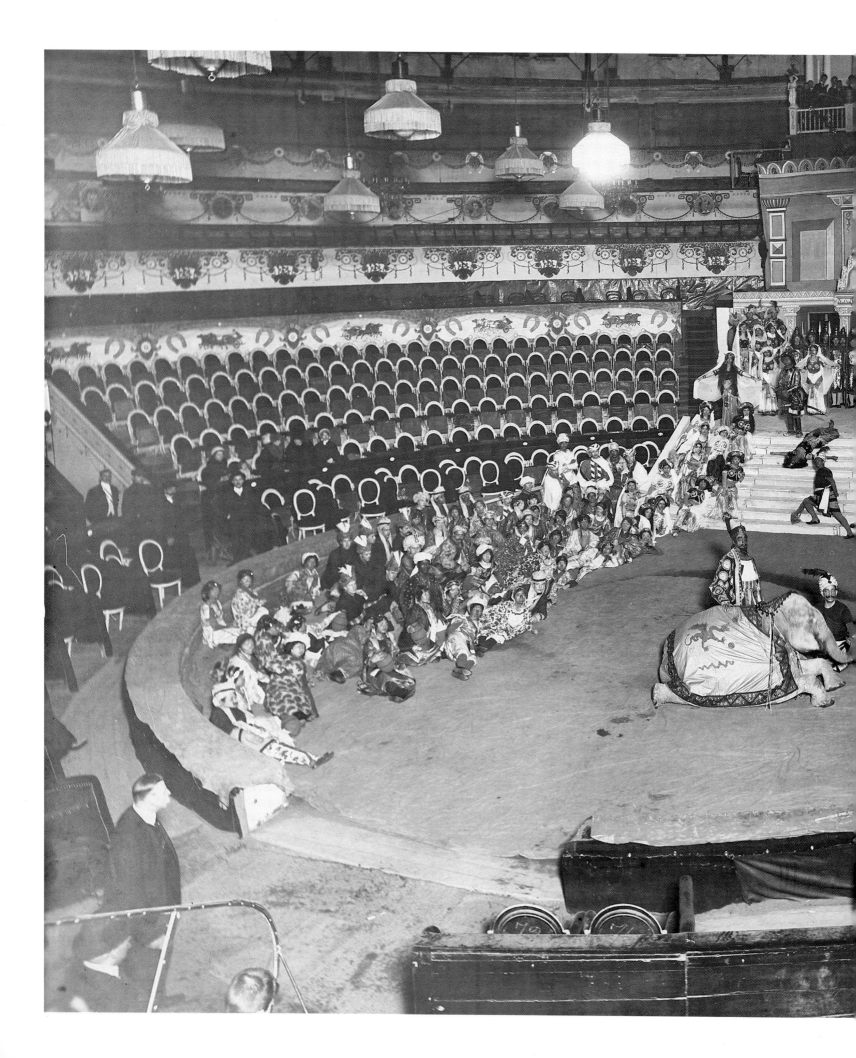

Ciniselli Circus. Rehearsal. 1910s

ABOVE:

A participant in wrestling contest in France being interviewed. 1912

CENTER:

Animal trainer Vladimir Leonidovich Durov. 1911

A circus actor, clown, and outstanding animal trainer noted for his exceedingly gentle handling of the animals, Vladimir Durov (together with his brother Anatoly) was the founder of the Russian school of animal training.

OPPOSITE:

**Façade of the building of the
Society for the Promotion of
Arts. 38 Bolshaya Morskaya
Street. 1912**

The Society for the Promotion of
Arts contained a Drawing School,
the director of which was Nicholas
Roerich, a famous painter and cultural figure. He enlisted the services
of talented artists and architects
such as V. Mathé, I. Bilibin,
N. Samokish, V. Shchuko, and
A. Shchusev.

ABOVE:

**Nicholas (Nikolai
Konstantinovich) Roerich,
artist, scientist, and philosopher. 1910s**

"The very technique of his painting,
oils, and especially tempera, was
very solid and accomplished, but
his art stood apart in The World
of Art. Roerich was an enigma to
everyone." *Mstislav Dobuzhinsky*

Mikhail Petrovich Botkin, member of the Academy of Arts. 1913

The sculptor Amandus Adamson. 1913

Amandus Adamson designed the bronze decorations for the building at
28 Nevsky Prospekt erected in 1902–04 and designed by architect
P. Y. Suzor for Singer, the American sewing-machine company. Adamson
also designed the sculptural decorations for the Troitsky (Trinity) Bridge
in Petersburg.

The painter and graphic artist Konstantin Andreyevich Somov. 1910s

The Russian illustrated art magazine *Mir Iskusstva* (1899–1904), founded by Diaghilev and advocating the search for new forms, brought together many outstanding artists including Alexander Benois, Leon Bakst, Evgeny Lanceray, Nicholas Roerich, Valentin Serov, Mikhail Nesterov, Mikhail Vrubel, Konstantin Korovin, and Isaak Levitan, to name a few. Mstislav Dobuzhinsky wrote about Konstantin Somov, a member of the group: "The extraordinarily intimate nature of his work, his mysterious imagery, and a sense of sad humor and the 'Hoffman' romanticism he then espoused stirred me profoundly and gave me a glimpse of a strange world that was akin to my vague yearnings."

**Left to right: the writer Kornei Ivanovich Chukovsky
(N. V. Korneichukov), the artist Ilya Efimovich Repin, Natalia
Borisovna Nordman-Severova.**
Repin's Penaty summer place in Kuokkala. 1910

A frequent guest of the famous Russian Realist painter Ilya Repin in Penaty,
Kornei Chukovsky wrote some interesting reminiscences directly linked with
this photograph. "He [Repin] utterly detested Filosofov and Benois, two of the
members of The World of Art. When, on the day of Tolstoy's death, the photographer Bulla took his picture with a black-framed issue of *Rech* (*Speech*) in his
hands, he forbade the exhibition of the photo because the egregious Filosofov
was a member of the *Rech* staff."

Alexander Alexandrovich Alekhine, the future world chess champion. 1909

"We are witnessing a miracle and a mystery," wrote grand master S. Tartakover. "The behests and hopes of the great Chigorin are at last coming true. If Morphy was the poet of chess, Steinitz the fighter, Lasker the philosopher and Capablanca a wonder machine, Alekhine, in keeping with the ever soul-searching, tormented Russian spirit, is more and more showing himself to be a seeker after truth in chess." According to grand master Salo Flor, Alekhine was "the absolute ideal who excelled equally in all the stages of the game."

St. Petersburg Chess Club. 53 Nevsky Prospekt. Early 1900s

Interest in chess in Petersburg at the turn of the century was tremendous. Amateur associations existed at just about every college, gymnasium, and large business in the city.

ABOVE, LEFT:

**The photographer Karl
Karlovich Bulla. 1904–06**

"The veteran photographer and il-
lustrator K. K. Bulla, 54 Nevsky
Prospekt, Petersburg. Provides topi-
cal photographs for illustrated magazines. Photographs everything you
wish, everywhere regardless of ter-
rain or interiors by day and by
night, with artificial lighting." This
was how the famous Petersburg
photographer Karl Bulla advertised
his business in newspapers. He
came to the capital as a twelve-year-
old boy, rose from a humble ap-
prentice to official photographer to
His Imperial Majesty's Court, and
founded a whole dynasty of first-
class professionals. Most of the photographs in this book come from his
studio.

ABOVE, CENTER:

**Exhibition of Karl Bulla's
work. 1912**

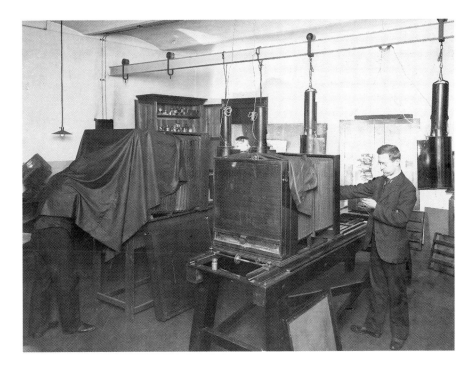

LEFT:
A group of photographers setting out to take pictures. Krasnoye Selo. 1902

ABOVE:
In a photo shop. 1900s

**Central Technical Drawing
School of Baron Stieglitz.
Grand Hall of the Museum.
9 Solianoi Lane. 1904**

The Central Technical Drawing
School aimed at improving the aes-
thetics of industry was founded in
Petersburg in 1879 with funds provided by Alexander Stieglitz, a
major financier. It offered classes in
majolica, decorative painting, etch-
ing, painting from life, prints, painting on porcelain and fabrics, uphol-
stery, etc.

OVERLEAF:

**Floating Exhibition of
the Imperial Russian Fire-
Fighting Society at the
Palace Embankment.
1910s**

**The interior of the Ekaterinhof Palace
(has not survived). 1903**

Conceived as a miniature estate, Ekaterinhof Palace (named after Peter I's wife, Ekaterina, or Catherine) was founded in 1711 together with a park to commemorate Russia's first naval victory in the Northern War when on May 12 (April 30 o.s.), 1703, two Swedish ships were captured in the mouth of the Fontanka River. In 1740 a second floor was added to the palace in which twenty-one rooms were later occupied by a museum.

ABOVE:
Ekaterinhof Palace (has not survived). 1900s

OPPOSITE:
The "American Hills" (switchback) in the Field of Mars. 1895

ABOVE:
Roundabout in the Field of Mars. 1890s

A group of figure skaters at the Skating Rink (has not survived) in the Field of Mars. 1911
Two facilities for roller-skating were built in 1910; one was in the Field of Mars and the other in Kamenno-Ostrovsky Prospekt.

Horse race on the Semionovsky Parade Ground. 1910

The history of this place is closely linked with that of the oldest Russian guard regiment, the Semionovsky, which took part in all the palace coups in the eighteenth century. As early as 1739 Empress Anna Ioannovna granted it large lots of land "beyond the Fontanka." Founded in 1860, the Society of the Lovers of Winter Horse Racing (from 1903 the Imperial St. Petersburg Society for the Promotion of Race Horse Breeding) established a racecourse on the eastern part of the ground. The first races were held on January 11, 1881 (December 28, 1880 o.s.). In addition to races, from 1884 the hippodrome was used for bicycle races and, from 1893, for football matches.

So much for the social and sporting history of the Semionovsky Parade Ground. Its other story is far more closely tied in with the history of Russia, although the association was often grim and tragic.

Here, in the Semionovsky, many courageous Russian revolutionaries who had challenged autocracy were executed during the nineteenth century. In 1849 it was the scene of the cruel charade in which a group of socialists from the circle of Mikhail Petrashevsky — among whom was Fiodor Dostoyevsky — were led to believe they would be executed by firing squad.

In 1881 the People's Will revolutionaries, who assassinated Alexander II, were executed here. Among them was a woman, Sophia Perovskaya. The execution most probably took place in the western part of the ground, as the eastern part was already being arranged for horse races.

The list of martyrs who died on the Semionovsky Parade Ground goes on and on.

Aviation Week at the Kolomiazhsky Hippodrome. Airman Bulganov (in helmet) and engineer Ya. M. Gikkel (sitting). April–May, 1910

One of the first Petersburg ice-hockey teams after a match in the Field of Mars. 1913

Cyclists on a three-seat bicycle. 1900s

Crew of a race car in the outskirts of Petersburg. 1910s

ABOVE:

Fashionable women of Petersburg. 1900s

A ball at the house of Countess Shuvalova. 1900s

Procession with a cross.
Apraksin Dvor. 1912

People promenading along Palace Embankment. Early 1900s

A farewell to St. Petersburg: soldiers going to the trenches of the Great War, the last, fatal war of the empire. 1914

All great empires were eventually eroded by the problems they could not solve and the unrest of their people, and often they crumpled in warfare. The first decades of the twentieth century, and especially the years of the Great War, saw the wreck of the four great modern empires: the German, the Austro-Hungarian, the Turkish, and the Russian, and the great city on the Neva entered a new era.

J Brooks

Anderson County Library
300 North McDuffie Street
Anderson, South Carolina 29622
(864) 260-4500

Belton, Honea Path, Iva,
Lander Regional, Pendleton,
Piedmont, Powdersville,
Westside, Bookmobile